POCKET IMA

Kirkcaldy
Remembered

Sailor's Walk, *c.*1910

POCKET IMAGES

Kirkcaldy
Remembered

Kirkcaldy Civic Society

NONSUCH

Kirkcaldy Esplanade, c.1930. The sea wall was completed in 1923.

First published 1999
This new pocket edition 2007
Images unchanged from first edition

Nonsuch Publishing Limited
Cirencester Road, Chalford,
Stroud, Gloucestershire, GL6 8PE
www.nonsuch-publishing.com

Nonsuch Publishing is an imprint of NPI Media Group

British Library Cataloguing in Publication Data.
A catalogue record for this book is available from the British Library.

ISBN 978-1-84588-386-7

Typesetting and origination by Nonsuch Publishing Limited
Printed in Great Britain by Oaklands Book Services Limited

Contents

Introduction

'A larger, more populous and better built town ... than any on this coast'.
(Daniel Defoe, 1660–1731)

Kirkcaldy, on the coast of central Fife, is one of Scotland's least appreciated large towns, and deserves to be more well-known for its fine buildings, long history and extraordinarily important cultural heritage. Despite many subsequent changes, Defoe's eighteenth-century description still holds true today. Numerous industries and occupations have come and gone, at times with bewildering speed, while fleeting images of others have been set in context for the Millennium by the members of Kirkcaldy Civic Society in this nostalgic volume.

When given to Dunfermline church in 1075, the place name was recorded as Kirkcaladunt, possibly deriving from Caer Caledonii–'Castle of the Caledonians'. A few coins prove local Roman connections, most likely with the Roman fort across the Firth of Forth at Inveresk. The old local name Dunnikier, 'Castle of the Fort' in Gaelic, may refer to another Roman fort, the possible source of the rectangular layout of nearby Pathhead (once known as Dunnikier). Also standing on this coastal promontory between Kirkcaldy and Dysart, a tiny historic burgh only two kilometres to the east, is Ravenscraig Castle, a Royal artillery fort of 1460–1461. Just west of the town is the site of the Dark Ages Battle of Raith, another hilltop estate that gets its name from the Irish-Scots Rath or 'Fort'. Eventually in 1694 the mansion of Raith House was built there, and in 1883 the name was adopted by the local football team, Raith Rovers.

Early religious schisms may also explain the name Kirkcaldy as 'Kirk of the Culdees', or Sons of God, men who followed the gentle Columban tradition here and elsewhere but were anathema to the authoritarian Abbot of Dunfermline, who built an outstation or hall nearby to keep an eye on them; hence Abbotshall.

Kirkcaldy, on its south-eastwards facing bay, was well placed to serve its rural hinterland with North Sea and Baltic trade, as commerce grew along a road linking the early bridges at the mouths of two burns. Only three kilometres away, beyond the Tiel Burn, was Balwearie, birthplace in 1214 of the international scholar and translator Michael Scot. Kirkcaldy's Old Kirk was consecrated in 1244 and St Serf's at Dysart in 1245 as early ports and, in exploiting the local coal measures to evaporate salt, these two were long in rivalry.

In the fourteenth century, Dunfermline Abbey obtained a regality charter for Kirkcaldy from David II and, by the early sixteenth century, Kirkcaldy vessels traded with the Baltic. By 1560, grain mills turned beside the Den Burn at the East Bridge—they still do! Milling led to malting for brewing and distilling, for which a major maltings is still busy at Sinclairtown just north of Pathhead. By 1573 some twenty-three salt pans were at work locally. Kirkcaldy was evidently promoted in a lost charter, for it joined the Convention of Royal Burghs in 1574 and by 1583 held trading rights as far inland as Kinglassie. The previous year of 1582 saw the founding of a burgh school, where the famous writer Thomas Carlyle was later to teach.

In 1589 one of Scotland's finest ships, the Angel of Kirkcaldy, was hired by James VI to fetch his bride Anne from her home in Denmark. The Law family's contemporary Merchant House at the Port Brae contains a recently discovered ship mural that may well be of this vessel. The ashlar frontage of the house may have come from the Priory of Abbotshall, demolished after the Reformation except for its tall precinct wall that still shelters part of a private housing estate (an eighteenth-century church on a nearby eminence bears the name Abbotshall). Despite a tiny harbour, where medieval stonework still shows among the later concrete, Kirkcaldy's trade certainly prospered: grain was imported by 1618 and continental beer was imported by 1625, although the Kirkcaldy merchantman Blessing was captured in the Mediterranean by Turkish pirates in 1632!

When chartered again as a Royal Burgh in 1644, Kirkcaldy had some 3,000 people and in 1655 twelve of its 100 sailing vessels were large for the day (up to 100 tons.) In 1656 the traveller Richard Franck found Kirkcaldy 'pleasant, cockly ... built all with stone'. Mason work brought an Angus family by the name of Adam to the town. William Adam, born there in 1689, became Royal Mason for Scotland, designing many famous buildings and sired the even more famous architects—the Adam Brothers.

Kirkcaldy for long operated ferries to the Lothians, and coaches on a road linking the rival Kinghorn ferry with Falkland were running through the town by 1663. In that year Linktown of Abbotshall, which lined this road, was chartered as a Burgh of Barony with two annual fairs. One of these, the Links Market, has survived to the present day as a major spring funfair, the first annual gathering place of the Scottish Showmen's Guild. Kirkcaldy and its string of neighbours grew into what was for centuries known as the 'Lang Toun', though in the later twentieth century it has become triangular on plan.

The local manufacture of linens from flax began about the time of the Restoration in 1660, and became a major industry that led to the painted linen called floorcloth and later still to linoleum, developed by the Nairn family. Among the Nairns' many bequests to the town was a fine art gallery. Other early local industries included nail making, from which grew a Pathhead factory making nails and pins on a now forgotten site. Its fame was ensured when Scotland's most famous son, locally born pioneer-economist Adam Smith, cited this industry in his classic work of 1776, The Wealth of Nations. Ranked by American author Michael Hart as the thirtieth most influential person in world history, he is remembered in the town's Adam Smith Theatre.

Around 1790 wealthy James Oswald built a new Dunniker House well inland. Away from Pathhead and the growing town, this and other historic houses are now hotels. Shipbuilding, whaling, marine engineering, iron founding, potteries, carpet weaving, electric tramways and in the last half-century telephone exchange manufacture and numerous other industries grew, prospered, and together with much of the once massive linoleum industry, ultimately failed. Dysart lost its burgh status in 1930 but still keenly nurtures its traditional independence and has another story to tell.

Trading was for centuries expressed through the now regrettably defunct port and later by way of busy but now vanished railway yards and sidings, while locally trained rail surveyor Sandford Fleming emigrated to Canada, earned a knighthood for his famed work in communications and invented Standard Time. Centres of bus and road transport still thrive, as do substantial modern shopping centres, both in and adjacent to the traditional High Street, at Sinclairtown and controversially at the Central Fife Retail Park. Education embraces some of Fife's leading secondary schools, and the growing Fife College of Higher Education has adapted striking industrial buildings to modern needs. There is also a College of Nursing and Midwifery.

Printing, furniture manufacture and industrial building fabrication carry on, and linens are still made at Sinclairtown, north of Pathhead. Linoleum is enjoying a comeback among more modern types of floor coverings made by the town's best-known firm, Forbo-Nairn, now in Swiss ownership. The once notorious smell of linseed oil is now largely a memory—occasionally just a whiff escapes!

The Royal Burgh of Kirkcaldy, with a population of 47,400 in 1997, sadly vanished in 1975 and its sandstone faced Town House, completed in 1957, became the centre for Kirkcaldy District Council. Some further reorganisation into the all-embracing Fife Council was implemented in 1996 when the building continued in local government as the civic centre of Central Fife.

It is perhaps fitting that we finish with the words of Thomas Carlyle to describe the town: 'The beach of Kirkcaldy in summer twilight, a mile of the smoothest sand, with one long wave coming on gently, steadily, and breaking into a gradual explosion beautifully sounding, and advancing, ran from the South to the North, from the West Burn to Kirkcaldy Harbour, a favourite scene beautiful to me still in the faraway'.

Carlyle continued to remark that 'The Kirkcaldy population were a pleasant, honest kind of fellow mortalism, something of the quietly fruitful good old Scotch in their words and way'.

This is still true today.

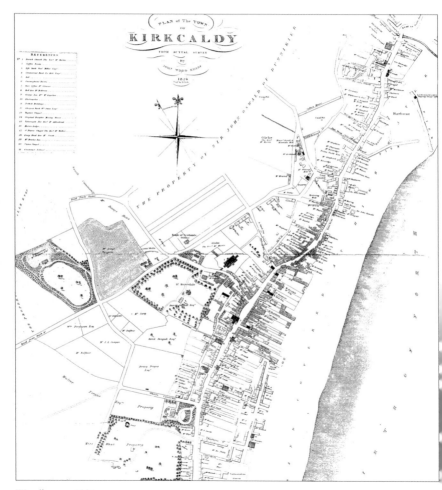

Wood's map, 1824.

One

People, Famous
and not so Famous

Many people born in Kirkcaldy have become famous like Adam Smith, Robert Adam or Sir Sandford Fleming. Others have been famous in Kirkcaldy like Marjory Fleming and Michael Nairn, and many other less well-known people have contributed much to Kirkcaldy's heritage.

Adam Smith 1723–1790. Adam Smith, the only child of Adam Smith, Controller of Customs, and Margaret Douglas of Strathhendry Castle, was born in 1723 only a few months after his father died. He wrote his famous book *The Wealth of Nations* while living in a house at 220 High Street with gardens that stretched down to Sands Road and the shore. The house was demolished in 1834 and later rebuilt. Adam Smith was a professor in Glasgow and then became a tutor to the young Duke of Buccleugh, travelling throughout Europe, after which he spent nine years in Kirkcaldy. It is said that he was so engrossed in thought one Sunday morning that he wandered down his garden path in his night-clothes onto Sands Road and along the Turnpike Road, only coming to his senses when he heard the church bells ringing and found himself in Dunfermline! Adam Smith was later appointed Controller of Customs for Scotland, like his father, and moved to Edinburgh, where he died in 1790. He is buried in Canongate Churchyard.

Robert Adam 1728-1792. Robert Adam was born in Gladney House, Kirkcaldy in 1728, second of four sons and six daughters. His father William Adam was a famous architect in his own right who was employed in building forts to control the Highlanders, as well as grand homes like Hopetoun House. William formed a partnership with William Robertson in Linktown, establishing the Brick and Tile Works and building Gladney House in 1711. He married William's daughter Mary and lived in Gladney House for several years before the family moved to Edinburgh. William Adam kept his links with Fife by building Blairadam House near Kelty, which is still inhabited by Adam descendants. The house is fairly plain as none of the family had the time or the cash for their country house. Robert went to the Burgh School in Kirkcaldy and later on a Grand Tour of Europe. He had a great flair for building and designing elaborate country houses. His brothers, John and James, were also well-known architects. Robert never married. He died in 1792 and is buried in Westminster Abbey.

Gladney House, built in 1711 by William Adam.

Provost Michael Beveridge 1836–1890. Michael Beveridge was born in Kirkcaldy in 1836 and died of pneumonia when serving as Provost of Kirkcaldy in 1890. Around 1870 he built Beechwood, a big house, and one of four at what was then the top of the town. The other houses were Forth Park, Kilmany, now Morningside, and Marchmont. Beechwood was home to Polish soldiers during the War and in 1945 was sold to the Royal British Legion. It is now part of a complex of luxury apartments. Michael Beveridge was married twice but had no children. In order to recognise the greatness of Adam Smith and to mark the occasion of 100 years since his death, Provost Michael Beveridge set up a memorial fund that resulted in the opening of the Adam Smith Halls and Beveridge Library by Andrew Carnegie in 1899, nine years after Beveridge had died. In his will, Provost Beveridge had left the people of Kirkcaldy £50,000 for a park and a library.

Bandstand in the Beveridge Park. The Beveridge Park was opened by Provost Michael Beveridge's widow in 1892. The bandstand later vanished around 1959. Note the efficient grasscutters at the time!

Thomas Carlyle 1795–1881. Thomas Carlyle was born in Ecclefechan in 1795, the son of a stonemason. He came to Kirkcaldy and taught in the Burgh School for two years from 1816–1818, lodging at a house in Kirk Wynd that was sadly demolished in favour of the Trustees Savings Bank. He was a good friend of Edward Irving, another teacher in Kirkcaldy. Irving later became a famous preacher, who was to have preached in the Old Parish Church on Sunday 15th June 1828. Tragically, the congregation moved forward on his arrival in order to get a good view, and the gallery collapsed killing twenty-eight people. Thomas Carlyle married Jane Welsh from Haddington, but there were no children. Her cousin Walter Welsh was the minister at Auchtertool church from 1842–1880, and the couple often visited the village five miles from Kirkcaldy. Money was tight for many years but the Carlyles finally moved to London where he became known as the 'Sage of Chelsea' and wrote profusely. Thomas died in 1881 and is buried in Ecclefechan Kirkyard beside his family, while his wife is buried in Haddington Church beside her father.

Thomas Carlyle's lodging house, Kirk Wynd.

Anna Buchan (O. Douglas) 1875–1947. O. Douglas was the *nom de plume* of Anna Buchan, sister of John Buchan, a well-known Scottish author. Anna was born in 1875, daughter of the Rev. John Buchan and Helen Masterton from Broughton. The family came to Pathhead, Kirkcaldy, from Perth when Rev. Buchan became minister of Pathhead West Church. At that time, the Manse was in Smeaton Road but it has since been demolished to make space for what was once the Fife Forge. Anna and Walter, her unmarried brother, looked after their parents in Peebles, while John became Governor General of Canada, where he died in 1940. Anna died in Peebles in 1947. There is a small Buchan Museum in the Old Free Church in Broughton where Anna's parents first met when Rev. John Buchan was standing in for the incumbent minister. Pathhead West Church was demolished to make way for the Ravenscraig flats in 1963.

Pathhead West Manse, Smeaton Road.

George and Joanna Elder. George Elder was a merchant who came from Leith and settled in Kirkcaldy. He married Joanna Haddo Lang in Leith and they had four sons and three daughters. George Jr was the first of the four sons to go to Australia, as captain of his father's ship *Minerva*, which upon arrival in Australia traded along the coast with essential supplies including rum and other spirits. He was followed by his three brothers and sister Joanna, who went as the bride-to-be of Richard (Barr) Smith. George Elder Sr named the house he built in Kirkcaldy Adelaide House, due to his strong links with Australia. The house was later renamed Wemyss Park and was demolished around 1937 to make way for the present Town House. Three sons returned from Australia and settled in Scotland, while Thomas, a bachelor, remained in Australia, later to become Sir Thomas Elder. He prospered in business, setting up the Elder Smith Company Limited with Robert Barr Smith. Thomas also helped to found and finance the University of South Australia in Adelaide. Joanna and Robert Barr Smith had a large family and prospered in South Australia.

Adelaide House.

Marjory Fleming 1803–1811. Marjory Fleming was born in 1803 at what is now 132 High Street, Kirkcaldy, the middle daughter of James Fleming and Isabella Rae. Her parents met at a ball given by Provost Walter Fergus in the Whyte House around 1794. Marjory was a very bright and precocious little girl and when the third daughter was expected she was sent to live with her cousin Isabella Keith in Edinburgh, where she was made a great fuss of and became very happy. Not only did she write poetry, but her cousin, who acted as her governess, made her keep a journal which has given a clear insight into a child's life at that time. After nearly three years in Edinburgh, Marjory returned to Kirkcaldy where she was not happy. She caught measles during an epidemic, and shortly after recovering came down with meningitis, from which she died in 1811, shortly before her ninth birthday. Marjory was buried in Abbotshall Churchyard and a special memorial was erected to her in 1937.

Rear of Marjory Fleming's House, 132 High Street. Marjory's home faced the sea. It is largely unchanged today but there is no public access to the rear.

Volunteers' Green, c.1880. Volunteers' Green was part of ground given to Kirkcaldy by the Charter of Charles I in 1644 as a place 'for drying and bleaching of linen and for recreation'. The original, nearly nine acres, had been eroded away until there was less than 0.75 of an acre. In 1860, Volunteers were formed all over the country as soldiers-in-waiting in case they should be required for war. At this time the Crimean War (1854–1856) had just finished and it was not known where or when the next conflict would occur. The leading men from the gentry and industry in the town became officers.

There were three companies in Kirkcaldy of the 1st Fife Royal Garrison Volunteers. Drilling was on Volunteers' Green from 1860 until 1901 when the Volunteers moved to Kinghorn. In 1923 the sea wall was built which separated Sands Road from the shore. The Green again became a drying green surrounded by a wall, but much neglected in appearance. A twice-weekly market was set up in 1976 but with so many objections that it was excluded by 1978. However, in 1992, Volunteers' Green was landscaped into a beautiful public garden.

Volunteers' Green with cannon on the sands; prior to 1901.

Home Guard, 1942. The Home Guard was formed during the Second World War and was recruited from men with reserved occupations, senior citizens and those too young to volunteer. It was different from the Territorials who were mostly called up to serve in the Armed Forces after war was declared. In the event of invasion the Home Guard was to defend our towns and villages and harass the enemy. They have been very well portrayed in the television series *Dad's Army*.

VAD Nurses. Many VAD (Voluntary Aid Detachment) nurses, although not fully trained, served with distinction at the front of battle during the First and Second World Wars. The VAD service still continued for a time after the war, ready to be mobilized if the need should arise.

Rev. Thomas Snoddy, 1885–1971. Rev. Thomas Snoddy was minister at Pathhead East Church (now Pathhead Parish) from 1922 until 1956. A native of Greenock, he played football for Greenock which helped to pay his way through college and entry to the ministry. He served in France during the First World War, later marrying and fathering three children, one of whom ran a pharmacy business in Kirkcaldy. Rev. Snoddy was a walker and walked all over Fife. He wrote several books giving the history and the stories of the places he walked through, including *Afoot in Fife* and *Tween Forth and Tay*. Thomas Snoddy was also a great admirer of Michael Bruce (1746–1767), a teacher and poet who died aged twenty-one at Portmoak and about whom he wrote several small books.

Kirkcaldy Burgh Police Benevolent Fund, 1900. 'This fund was administered to provide boots to poor and needy children not reached through ordinary channels of charity. Distressing cases of destitution are often brought to the notice of the police and the persons concerned abhor appealing to charity but the officers are able in the course of their duties and in strict privacy, to give a helping hand'. Todays police are still involved in such projects, but in a different way!

Two

Houses, Big and Small

Kirkcaldy has lost many of the big houses built between the end of the eighteenth century and the end of the nineteenth century, some owned by industrialists. Kirkcaldy has also lost many of the small terraced tenement houses built for the workers, usually two-roomed dwellings with a shared toilet. Many were tied houses and went with the job.

The Whyte House is a list B building under orders to be demolished to provide extra car parking space. However, few Kirkcaldy people have seen the house or know of its whereabouts as the ground has been sold off over the years, leaving the house surrounded by tall buildings with only a narrow lane leading in to a local bakery. The house was built around 1790 by Robert Whyte—at one time the Provost of Kirkcaldy. It has seen many famous families living here, among them the Drydales, Lockharts and Ferguses. It became the first Anthony's Temperance Hotel from around 1908 before conversion to four flats and offices of the local bakery after 1953, when Antony's Hotel moved to Gowrie House and the Rectory in West Albert Road. Both these houses were demolished to make way for the new Gowrie House Nursing Home which opened in 1995.

'The Lions' House', opposite the old Invertiel Free Church in the Links, was built in 1778 by David Methven of Linktown Potteries and was so named due to the two lions at the front door. The lions were made at the Linktown Pottery and looked like 'begging spaniels'. The house was demolished at the beginning of the twentieth century to make way for new Co-op buildings which closed in 1984, while the Lions are still somewhere in Perthshire. A pair of lions are to be found at the gates of Beveridge Park and were also probably made in the Linktown Potteries. They were gifted to the park by Daniel Hendry of Forth Park shortly before he died. His family did not welcome 'Daniel in the Lions' Den'. It was said that a ghost was seen several times in the garden of the Lions' House at the turn of the twentieth century and 'eventually passed a message to the Colonel living there.'

'The Lions' House' lions.

Balsusney House. Balsusney House was built around 1790 by John Jeffrey, a linen manufacturer who owned the nearby Balsusney linen works, which later became the head office of Barry, Ostlere and Shepherd and is now used by Fife Council. John Maxton from Crieff bought Balsusney House, which stood where the museum is today. The house was then purchased by Kirkcaldy Town Council before the start of the First World War with the purpose of conversion into a museum, but it was demolished after the war. John Nairn built the museum and art gallery, and later the library, as part of the war memorial in memory of his only son Ian and many others from Kirkcaldy, killed during the First World War.

St Mary's. St Mary's was bought by Michael Barker Nairn around 1880 and was the home of his daughter Catherine for over fifty years. Michael Barker Nairn moved to Rankeillor, near Cupar and in 1896 he bought Dysart House as a winter residence. In 1904 he was made a Baronet. Originally, St Mary's consisted of two storeys but it was extended by adding a third storey. Mrs Nairn lived nearby in the Priory, built around 1880, with her son Robert and her unmarried daughters, Euphemia and Isabella. St Mary's was eventually used by the sea cadets and was demolished around 1963.

Ravenscraig Castle. Ravenscraig Castle was built for defence by James II in 1460. He died before it was completed and it passed to the Earl of Caithness, William Sinclair, hence that part of Kirkcaldy became known as Sinclairtown. In the early seventeenth century, the Sinclairs built a mansion house nearby, The Hermitage, which went on fire in 1722 and was rebuilt as Dysart House. During the Civil War, the castle was broken into by Cromwell's troops, as it was being used as a granary at the time. The English Roundheads found both food and shelter. In 1971 Historic Scotland opened the castle to the public. It is still open without supervision.

Path House with Nairn's old offices on the left, c.1960. This is an old view of the Path House built by John Watson of Burntisland in 1692 and sold to Captain Oswald in 1702. It was originally known as Dunniker House and the round turret was added later. It is now a doctor's surgery. On the left of the photograph can be seen the red sandstone Grecian style offices of the Nairn Company that were built in 1903 and demolished when 'The Path' was widened in 1967. Polish soldiers were billeted here during the Second World War.

Above and right: Viewforth Towers. Viewforth Towers was built around 1790 by Robert Pratt, who, with Heggie was a linen manufacturer in Linktown. His name is still remembered in Pratt Street. Viewforth Towers had grounds stretching down to the shore with a lodge, stables, vinery and fine gardens. It had a tower, fourteen rooms, including two round ones, and may have been an Adam House. Towers were fashionable at the time, enabling the owner to watch for his sailing ships returning from the far seas. It became such a fashionable feature that many inland houses and families not owning ships often had mansion houses with towers. In 1880 Mr Thomson sold the house to Dr Curor and later it was sold to Kirkcaldy Labour Homes for a model-lodging house. When Viewforth Towers was demolished in 1958 to build eight-storey flats, a tunnel was found leading to the shore that may have had some use in the days of smugglers.

Marine Cottage. Marine Cottage was a lovely little cottage in the Links that was last inhabited by a Miss Mckay, whose father had been a local builder. She died around 1985 and the cottage was demolished a few years later.

Clay Pipe House. George Lowrie was a native of Leith who came to Kirkcaldy in 1895 with his brother William and set up a clay pipe business in Cowan Street. In 1906 they moved the business to Sands Road and lived in the Marine Cottage. Across the garden was Clay Pipe House, at the junction of Sands Road with Bute Wynd. This was where the clay pipes were manufactured. Clay from Cornwall, brought in by boat, was shovelled into the basement to mature before being ready to be fired into pipes. George Lowrie died in 1915 and his brother closed the business and left town. The building was then used to repair sacks before the days of plastic sacks, while the upper part was a hackle shop which closed in the 1940s. The buildings were demolished around 1990. Many people digging in their gardens in Kirkcaldy often come up with bits of long-discarded clay pipes.

Halley Houses, Bute Wynd/Links Street. The houses in Links Street at the corner of Bute Wynd belonged to the Halley family, who were dyers. George Halley came to Kirkcaldy from Leith in 1873 aged twenty and worked as a clerk in Walter Heggie's dyeworks which had been established in 1825. Heggie died in 1870 and his son continued for a short time before George Halley took over the works. In 1920 the works moved into Aytoun's empty mill in Nicol Street, eventually closing in 1984 after having had three generations of George Halleys.

Baron Baillie's House, Links Street. The Baron Baille's House was partly used as a jail when Linktown of Abbotshall was a Burgh of Barony, formed in 1663. The Baron Baillie acting for the Superior lived in this house, a tolbooth, with its forestairs and the jail below the house. Above was a bell that sadly was removed and is believed to be somewhere in South Africa. In 1876 Linktown, with other small burghs, became a part of the Royal Burgh of Kirkcaldy, and the house became a bookshop. It was demolished around 1965.

Dunnikier Colliery Cottages. Dunnikier Colliery Cottages were cottages owned by Dunnikier Colliery and housed miners from the Dunnikier Colliery and their families. The cottages were demolished in order to make way for the new fire station in 1937. The colliery closed after the General Strike in 1926 and part of the cobbled road leading off St Mary's Road is still there, leading to garages belonging to people nearby. Dunnikier Colliery or Pannie Pit was worked from 1881 by Walter Herd and was on lands belonging to the Oswalds of Dunnikier.

Lady Helen Cottage, Raith Gates. Lady Helen Cottage was named after Lady Helen, wife of Lord Novar, who was at one time Governor General of Australia. It was built at Raith Gates and donated by Lady Helen as a home for two district nurses. After Raith Gates Eventide Home was opened in 1976 the cottage was abandoned and became surrounded with vegetation and weeds until it had to be demolished.

Goodsir Terrace, Nether Street. At the top of Nether Street was a terrace of cottages demolished when the road was widened with the building of multi-storey flats in 1967. This was Goodsir Terrace.

Terraced tenements, Nicol Street. Nicol Street was once a densely populated street with blocks of terraced tenements about three storeys high. Here large families lived in cramped and overcrowded conditions, sharing a toilet. These houses were part of 'Newtown', built around 1870 when Kirkcaldy was overflowing into Linktown and housing was required for the workers in the many linen mills. Newtown was renamed Nicol Street after Nicol, a local linen manufacturer. The old houses were demolished and new homes built in Nicol Street from 1970–1975. Peggie's Public House is also seen in this view.

Coal Wynd and High Street Corner. The houses here were demolished when Coal Wynd was widened in 1989. Coal Wynd was so named as coal came down here from the Dunnikier Colliery for export from ships at the harbour. Along the High Street with its public houses were once two lanes, Stewart's Lane and Coldwell Lane, connecting with the Coal Wynd. To the right was Beattie's Mother's Pride Bakery.

21–40 Oswald Road. New local authority houses were built on Oswald Road around 1950. These old houses were very poor quality, built for the workers of the potteries or nearby linen mills at the end of the nineteenth century. The houses had outside stairs, wash houses and toilets, both shared by several families. Oswald Road was named after the Oswalds of Dunnikier and is on land that originally belonged to the family, although land on the other side of Rosslyn Street belonged to the Earl of Rosslyn. Oswald Road connects with Rosslyn Street.

Three

Shops and Streets

Formerly known as the 'Lang Toun', Kirkcaldy has developed over the years from being long and narrow to being nearly as broad as it is long. The town was well served with shops, both multiples and a large number of long-serving family businesses. People came from all parts of Fife and further afield to shop in Kirkcaldy. These days the shops are moving to the outskirts of the town and into shopping precincts.

Junction of Whytescauseway with High Street, c.1905.

High Street (West End). Prominent on the right is the spire of the Abbotsrood church, closed in 1949 when the congregation moved to Hayfield Road. This former church, the spire of which was removed for safety reasons, had many uses over the years and at present is the Global video shop. Note the sign for Neilson Bros, once a bicycle shop and a forerunner of Neilson's Garage that used to stand where Safeway's supermarket was. There is an interesting advertisement on the tramcar for Reid Bros Dentists. The spire of West End Congregational Church is on the left.

Whyte's Causeway. This shows a tramline junction at the corner of Whyte's Causeway and the High Street. On the right is Heggie's Linen Mill and below Hill Street are the buildings replaced by Burton's in 1937. Whyte's Causeway (now Whytescauseway) was so named due to its origin from land once part of the Whyte House.

High Street from Whytehouse Avenue, looking east. Graham's china shop was a well-known meeting place for lads and lassies as the buses from the countryside stopped there. J. & A. Grieve, a popular outfitters, is on the right. The premises of Mathieson's shoes show Burton's buildings. The Plaza Ballroom above that was opened on the corner by the Burton brothers in 1937.

Graham's china shop corner. Other shops along this side of the High Street in 1948 were Scottish Wool and Hosiery, J. Henderson, butcher (still there) and Noble the newsagent. Standing in Graham's china shop window are some of the staff, among them Tommy, Alice, Betty, Marjorie and Hero. The 'boss' is standing at the main door. A bowl of fresh water was always placed in Graham's doorway for thirsty dogs.

High Street from Whytescauseway, 1907. Shops around here included David Michie; Italian warehouseman James Irss; and Buchan's Beehives selling umbrellas, hats and caps. The building on the left belonged to J. McBean before Burton's was built on this corner.

Kirkcaldy High Street, centre, c.1950. There were numerous shops in the centre of the High Street that have now disappeared—Burt's Bookshop and Travel Agent; Rennie the Grocer; Barnet and Morton, ironmonger; Sang Seedsman; Hepworth's; Carr's and A.T. Hogg's shoe shop; and Grinton, tobacconist.

Right: An advert from A. Currie & Son, Scotch Whisky Merchants, from a map produced in the early part of the century.

Below: High Street looking towards the Port Brae, *c.*1910. On the right can be seen the entrance to 220 High Street, Adam Smith House, with its two magnificent Ionic columns. Although the original building is no longer there, this is the site where Adam Smith lived and wrote *The Wealth of Nations*. A few yards beyond is Adam Smith Close, previously named Halkett's Close. This part of the High Street was well served with newsagents, banks and chemists early in the twentieth century. The buildings above the shop-fronts have changed little.

Left: Co-operative Store, the High Street. This Co-operative building was built at the corner of Oswald Wynd and High Street in 1903. Sadly, the building went on fire in 1975 and the present building was erected on the site. The High Street Co-operative closed in 1992.

Below: Kirkcaldy, East End. Shops at the east end (Port Brae) of the High Street included Johnny Lena's fish shop, once famous for its fish teas. The shop became the Jumbo Restaurant but has been purchased as part of the Merchant's House, which has completely transformed this building to its sixteenth-century appearance as one of the oldest houses in Kirkcaldy. While the outside has been restored nothing has yet been done to the inside. Other shops that were once in the area were the Harbour Post Office and Thom the butcher, later to become a fish shop.

Above: Kirkcaldy, Station Road/Sang Road. A. Murdoch, sculptor, sits on the corner with Hogarth's Mill in the background. 101 Café and Candy Corner, newsagent, now stand on this corner.

Below: Balsusney Road. James Haig stands outside outside his grocer shop. When this photograph was taken he was told off for not putting on a clean apron.

St Clair Street, looking up from Nether Street/Dysart Road. On the left is Pathhead West Church, demolished in 1963 to make way for a fifteen-storey block of flats.

Mid Street, Pathhead. The house on the left shows crow-stepped gables and forestairs, the latter having been mostly demolished to make more road space. The shop on the right was a newsagents and there was also a fish and chip shop along here. Most of these buildings have disappeared.

Pathhead and Sinclairtown Reform Co-operative Society. This building was in Viewforth Street and led into large premises with a dairy. The building lay empty for many years and was demolished when the blocks of flats at Orkney Place were built. The first Co-operative building was in Commercial Street, as was the large extension and head office. Various Co-op branches opened over the years and eventually amalgamated as Kirkcaldy and District Co-operative Society—'Oh the memories of waiting in the queue for the Store Dividend'.

Opening of a new branch, 1903. The crowd must be waiting for some bargains at this opening of a new Pathhead and Sinclairtown Reform Society branch. It is thought that this was the St Clair Street branch, now the Happy Chinese Garden restaurant.

JUNCTION ROAD, KIRKCALDY.

Above: St Clair Street. A. Neilson, butcher, whose premises were in the row of shops opposite Sinclairtown Station.

Left: Corner of Junction Road and St Clair Street. Paterson's shop is now a takeaway sandwich shop, while Harley's on the other corner now sells carpets. Ireland's linen factory is in the background. The houses on Lorne Street corner were demolished to make way for flats and a car park. Note the photograph was taken before D. Grant, fish merchant, opened his shop on the left.

Looking up St Clair Street from Junction Road, c.1905. There are shops on both sides of the road. On the left is the Methodist Church, opened here in 1888 to try and combat the heavy drinking habits of workers in the area. Beyond is Peter Greig's linen factory. The chimney has been demolished but the factory is one of two linen factories left in Fife. The tramcar carries a typical local advert.

Dysart Co-operative, Rosslyn Street, Gallatown. This building was opened in 1895 and the stone shows the three tigers (or cats) with shuttles in their mouths, symbol of the Gallatown Weavers. The same symbol is found on the graves of some master weavers in Pathhead Feuars' Graveyard.

Dysart Co-operative, Rosslyn Street, Gallatown. Staff from the Dysart Co-operative, Rosslyn Street grocer's shop, on parade for a photograph. The large number of staff was needed to weigh out butter, sugar, biscuits, etc. to customer requirements. Maggie Shields is one of the ladies who worked in this particular shop.

Rosslyn Street, Gallatown, 1910s. This view is looking down Rosslyn Street. The shops on the right are Miss Greenaway the chemist and Miss Stewart the newsagent, and further down is the Royal Oak. Beyond that is the gable end of Doctor's Row which it is hoped will soon be renovated.

Four

Schools

In the year 1582 a Kirkcaldy minister, Dr David Spens, was contracted to teach a grammar school in Kirkcaldy. A song school was already in existence in the town and it supported the new grammar school. There was no school building, however, and the pupils were taught in the minister's house. In 1587 the council discussed building a schoolhouse and the Presbytery records of 1636 mention a school. In 1790 the council examined three candidates for the position of second teacher in the grammar school. Each candidate at their interview had to read a page from Milton and The Spectator and to 'sing a tune of music'! The Industrial Revolution in the 1800s brought many changes to Kirkcaldy, including the building of new schools. A successful linen manufacturer by the name of Robert Philp executed a trust deed whereby he bequeathed effects which amounted to the sum of £74,626,17s 6d to create a foundation for the education of 400 children. Not only did the boys and girls receive their education free, but school books, requisites and clothing from bonnets to boots were provided. For a number of years the boys on leaving received a sum of money as a start to buy tools, etc. Robert Philp died in 1824.

The Linktown School (above) had the figure of Robert Philip on top of the front gable. The school opened in 1828 and closed in 1890 as did the other Philp schools due to the passing of the Education (Scotland) Act of 1872. The building was used as a community hall and later as a school for special pupils. It was demolished in 1966. Robert Philp's second cousin, Dr John Philp (Philip), a South African missionary, had added an 'i' to his

name and this is what spurred Robert to leave all his money to educating the poor. He said, 'if ma name is 'na guid enough for him then neither is ma siller'.

Left: Robert Philp, who was born in Kirkcaldy, began making his money by travelling around the home weavers, collecting cloth and selling at markets. He later decided that there was more money to be made in manufacturing and so bought the West Mills in Mill Street, a spinning, dying and bleaching works. He was a bachelor and died in 1824—his grave is in the Old Parish Church graveyard and tells of his bequest to Kirkcaldy. A very touching custom for many years prevailed in connection with the Philp schools. All the pupils (known as Philpers) benefiting from the Philp Trust met on the anniversary of the testator's death and walked in procession to the churchyard; each, in turn, depositing a rose on his grave, while receiving a bun to eat in exchange.

Below: Sinclairtown School was very grand-looking from the outside. Inside, there was no heating except for a coal fire fed by the pupil's contributions. In 1900 Michael Nairn & Co. acquired this school as well as the nearby Dunnikier Free Church but the company did not demolish the buildings; instead they built around them. When the Nairns buildings were demolished in 1964 the school and church were intact, only to be demolished later.

Right: In 1896, Peter Purves School, described as a 'sabbath school', stood in the Linktown on Sands Road (today the Esplanade). Peter Purves was born in Dundee in 1799 and came to Kirkcaldy as a gardener in 1822. He became an Elder of Bethelfield Church (now Linktown Church) in Nicol Street, was very well read, highly intelligent and wrote poetry. In 1831 he was persuaded by some of the other Elders to open a school. He also covered religious teaching in the Philp schools.

Below: Adam Smith (economist and author of *The Wealth of Nations*) and Robert Adam (the famous architect and designer) both attended the Burgh School. The school was situated in Hill Street between 1725 and 1843 and a wall plaque marks the site today. Thomas Carlyle, the famous writer who became known as 'The Sage of Chelsea', taught in this school. He was appointed as the Master in 1816 at a salary of £80 and stayed in Kirkcaldy until 1818. Eventually the school was considered too small and larger premises were required.

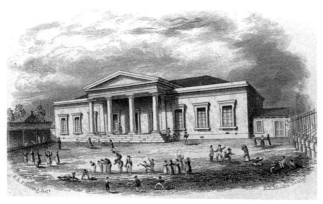

Left: In 1843 the new Burgh School was built in St Brycedale Avenue replacing the old school in Hill Street. Constructed in the 'Greek' style it cost £1,500 to build. In a Government list published in 1872 the school was classed as a 'higher class school conspicuous by its history and excellent results'.

Below: Sir Michael Barker Nairn, linoleum manufacturer and chairman of the Kirkcaldy School Board, gifted to the town a new school which was built on the site of the existing Burgh School. In erecting the new school the old one had to be kept in mind as the inhabitants of Kirkcaldy had become used to the outline of the old building. The façade of the old school was therefore reconstructed on the first floor of the new school, which cost upwards of £10,000. A bust of Sir Michael Barker Nairn was placed above the main entrance to the hall to remind pupils of their benefactor. A feature of the school was a speaking tube system connecting the Rector's room to the classrooms. There was a fire in the school on 9 August 1905.

Right: Main Block, Templehall Junior Secondary School. Phase one of Templehall Junior Secondary School was built in 1952 on the new local authority housing estate as a semi-permanent building. In 1957 a permanent brick wing was built containing art and science rooms, a swimming pool, gym and hall. In 1972, when comprehensive education was introduced, the building became the Junior building of Kirkcaldy High School. When the High School combined

the two units into one campus the Junior building was surplus to requirements and was demolished in 1997 to make way for a new housing development.

Below: Gordon Brown, Chancellor of the Exchequer (back row, fourth from left) joins his fellow prefects (school year 1966/67) for a photograph to be published in the school magazine of which he was one of the editors and contributors. His father was the School Chaplain and the minister at St Brycedale Church.

Pathhead Primary School, 1913. The first Pathhead school was the subscription school, opened in 1863 and supported by the Pathhead Feuars Society. It was replaced by Pathhead Public School in 1891, a local authority built school that is shown above. The school site was acquired by Michael Nairn & Co. and a new school was opened in Cairns Street in 1915.

Pathhead Primary School in Cairns Street was destroyed by fire in 1990 and a new school was erected in 1991 on the same area of ground. Whilst the new school was under construction the pupils and teachers were sent to nearby schools until their new premises were ready.

Right: Private Robert Dunsire was a pupil of Pathhead School and received the Victoria Cross during the First World War, which he won for carrying wounded colleagues back from enemy lines. After a triumphant homecoming, he returned to France and was tragically killed in action in 1915, aged twenty-three. His name is that of the only VC winner on Kirkcaldy's War Memorial of over 1,000 names.

Below: Salvaged from the 1990 fire, the school's weather vane is now on display in the reception area of the rebuilt school. The unusual design shows a globe of the world, a dominie and his young pupils.

A Dunnikier Primary School class photographed in 1913.

Prior to the Second World War, Seaview School was in the High Street and was moved to St Ronan's, Bogily Road, during the war as there were no air raid shelters in the High Street. After the war the school moved into 'The Terrace', a house built by Mr Russell at the top of Oswald's High Street house garden. In 1962 the school moved to Loughborough Road and the house became a private nursery. The house was demolished in 1994 to make way for new flats.

Five

Sport and Leisure

In the past, leisure activities were nigh non-existent. Apart from travelling fairs and church socials, there was little available. In any case, people worked long hours for little money and did not have much time or energy left at the end of the day. A start in the right direction was made, however, in 1865 with the opening of the People's Club and Institute in premises on the High Street. It offered a meeting room, a billiard room, a subscription library and a reading room. Now, whether young, old or in-between, no one in Kirkcaldy has any excuse to be bored. Active or sedentary, most inclinations are catered for. Sport and leisure clubs abound for people wanting anything from physical exercise to gentle bowling on pleasant greens. There are also associations and organisations where one can pursue one's special interest. Kirkcaldy is also lucky in having an abundance of beautiful parks and gardens, all immaculately tended. In its heyday, Kirkcaldy boasted fourteen picture houses. Now it only has one cinema, the ABC (formerly the King's), which has three screens, and the Adam Smith theatre, which shows films, but not on a regular basis.

Beveridge Park.

PEOPLES' CLUB AND INSTITUTE.

ENTRANCE—TOP OF GLASSWORK STREET.

. THE MOST POPULAR PLACE OF · · AMUSEMENT IN TOWN. · · · ·

BILLIARDS. BAGATELLE. WHIST.
DOMINOES, &c., &c.

SPACIOUS READING-ROOM. –

All the Rooms are handsomely furnished.

FINEST AND LARGEST BILLIARD ROOM IN FIFE.

SIX SPLENDID TABLES.

THREEPENCE per Half-hour in daylight.
FOURPENCE ,, ,, gaslight.

TERMS OF MEMBERSHIP—

5 YEARLY; 1/6 QUARTERLY; 6d MONTHLY.

Single Admission, - ONE PENNY

131

The People's Club and Institute. This organisation was started in 1865. Its purpose: the social, moral, educational and recreational support and outlet of ordinary people. The building housing the club was obtained in 1882 and financed from general sources, including some Kirkcaldy employers. There was a meeting room for social gatherings and lectures, a billiard room, and later a subscription library and reading room. This enterprise proved to be so popular that the building had to be extended at the end of the nineteenth century. The club is run by its members and is still thriving.

Right: The Lido. This young woman braved the weather at the Lido in 1947. The amenity had been built in 1936 on the site of the old Invertiel Chemical Works. After its closure in 1953, Kirkcaldy had to wait until 1971, when the new indoor swimming pool was opened, much to the delight of those who like to swim all year round.

Below: Curling and Skating. After 1938, when an ice rink was opened, one no longer had to rely on the weather as shown in this photograph from 1870. The new rink offered skating, curling and ice-hockey, and also dancing in the 1940s and 1950s with music of the resident band (leader Simon Stungo, followed by Bill Duff), and visitors like Joe Loss, Ted Heath, Nat Gonella and Johnny Dankworth. There were also ice revues and pantomimes.

100. Curling at 1870

Raith Rovers. Founded in 1883, this club first played at Robbie's Park on the site of the present Beveridge Park, and later moved to Stark's Park, the ground of one of their rivals. They soon became Kirkcaldy's major team, winning five trophies in one season in the 1890s. Spectator interest developed rapidly due to the introduction of Saturday half-day working. One wag, in a club publication, wondered whether the rise of football had been down to the fact that public hanging ceased about then! Despite the inevitable ups and downs, the club has survived for over a century. In the 1992/93 season the club won the First Division Championship, and in 1994 won their first national trophy, the League Cup, with victory (on penalties over Celtic after a 2-2 draw at Ibrox Park.

The photograph above shows a team picture from 1957. From left to right, back row: Jackie Stewart (Coach). Willie Polland, Willie Knox, Charlie Drummond, Andy Young, Willie McNaught, Andy Leigh, Alex Whitelaw (Coach). Front row: Jimmy McEwan, Bernie Kelly, Ernie Copland, Jackie Williamson, Johnny Urquhart.

The famous half backs of the 1950s, Willie McNaught, Andy Leigh and Andy Young.

Kirkcaldy Cricket Club First XI, 1965. From left to right, back row: Rodger Eggins, Harry Cairns, Mike Tuckerman, John Walker, Ed Pitts, Gerry Green. Front row: George Hardy, John Irvine, John Cowie, Norman Watters, Jock Robertson, Mike McKenzie.

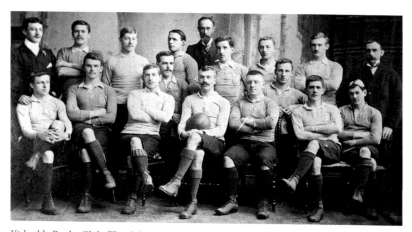

Kirkcaldy Rugby Club. The club was formed in 1873 and had its headquarters in the one-time 'National Hotel' on the High Street. The team initially played on ground at the top end of what is now Nicol Street, before the Beveridge Park was opened, and has long since moved into the park with an excellent pitch, clubhouse and changing rooms to match.

The Kirkcaldy and District Motorcycle Club. The club was formed in 1925, and during the 1930s ran races on Kirkcaldy beach. In 1948 the first motorcycle road races were held at Beveridge Park, where they continued until 1988. The above photograph shows riders getting ready for one such race. The circuit in the park is 1.375 miles long and 20ft wide. The club is still very active organising races and social events.

This is club member Jock Taylor, world sidecar champion in 1980. He was killed in 1982 during the Finnish Grand Prix—there is a memorial to him in Beveridge Park.

Beveridge Park, Kirkcaldy. Michael Beveridge was a linoleum manufacturer and former Provost of Kirkcaldy, who bequeathed money to the town upon his death in 1890. On 24 September 1892, the Beveridge Park was opened to the public. In this photograph, the gates and railings which partly surrounded the park are seen. These were removed during the Second World War along with many other metal items.

Ravenscraig Sands. Sir Michael Barker Nairn, who lived in Dysart House, gave the Ravenscraig Park to the Burgh of Kirkcaldy in 1929. This was part of his grounds, then known as 'The Three Trees Park'. Here the sands are seen with the park behind. This was for many years a popular bathing beach—note the raft moored off-shore where swimmers could take their ease. The park has beautiful panoramic views and in recent years a local church has held an open-air service here on Easter Sunday morning.

Raith Estate, Kirkcaldy. Ronald Crawford Munro Ferguson of Raith and Novar was Provost of Kirkcaldy from 1906–1914 (note the Provost's lamps). He was also an MP and Governor-General of Australia from 1914–1920. Later he became Viscount Novar and Secretary of State for Scotland until 1924. Unfortunately, there is no public access to the existing estate except by special permission.

Dunnikier Den, Kirkcaldy. Dunnikier Den runs from Dunnikier Way to the top of Dunnikier Road, where these magnificent gates have remained unchanged for nearly 100 years. Dunnikier House and Policies were bought by Kirkcaldy Burgh in 1935. The house is now a private hotel and the Den is open to the public as a right of way.

Above: The Mill Dam was artificially made by building a dam with a weir across the Tiel Burn. Water was used to supply power for the West Mill by means of a lade from the dam. Latterly, it became a beauty spot much favoured by walkers for many years. New EC regulations and concern for the safety of the dam, which was not owned by the Council, resulted in the dam being breached in 1989 and leaving a section of dangerous mud. After the dam was drained, the stonework became unsafe.

Left: Lovers on Johnny Marshall's Loan. What romantic memories this postcard must bring back to many Langtonians. Little is known about Johnny Marshall, except that he was a farrier who lived in this area. The lane was originally used for moving coal from the Lina pit to the harbour via Coal Wynd.

The public gardens in front of the library and museum house the War Memorial and have always been a credit to Kirkcaldy. Pictured is the Adam Smith Theatre, where many happy and informative hours have been spent by patrons over the years. To its left is William Robb's car showroom, which later became part of the Station Hotel. The whole building is now a nursing home.

On a warm, sunny day in the 1950s, the harbour steps were a popular meeting place for young and old for either a paddle or a dook. You would be sure to see a well-kent face among the hardier folk cavorting in the water or the idlers just soaking up the sun.

The Palace Cinema, Kirkcaldy. The Palace Cinema was built in Whytecauseway in 1913 as a variety theatre. In 1925, it became a cinema, and from 1929 showed 'talkies'. The Palace seated 1,000 with a cantilevered balcony that could seat 270. During the war years it was noted for its Ministry of Information Sunday Lectures. It was gutted by fire on 28th December 1945.

The Port Brae Cinema. The Port Brae Cinema opened in 1913, having been purpose-built on a vacant site between the High Street and what was then Sands Road, later known as the Esplanade after a sea wall was completed in 1923. It seated 616 people. In 1938 it was renamed the Old Opera House. It closed in 1942 and the building was demolished around 1949 to make way for a petrol station, which was later converted into a car showroom.

Six

Churches

The early Christian Church in Kirkcaldy was of the simple Culdee faith, but this changed when Queen Margaret, wife of King Malcolm Canmore, brought the Roman Catholic faith with her to Scotland, becoming the prime instigator of Dunfermline Abbey. At the time of the Reformation in 1548 John Knox destroyed the monastries and the churches, but was kind to Dunfermline Abbey, and slowly the Presbyterian Church began to establish itself. In 1733 the Secession occurred due to patronage, with the congregations wishing to appoint their own minister and not the Laird. There was a further split of this group in 1747 into Burghers and Anti-Burghers over the Burgess Oath and later to New Lichts and Auld Lichts. In 1843 there was the Disruption, with patronage again the dividing issue, and all the parish churches spawned free churches. Later,

Dunnikier Free Church. In 1747 this group broke away from the Burghers at the Bethelfield Secession Church and at first met in a malt barn near the harbour, but when it looked as if the wall was about to cave in, they moved into the Pathhead Feuars graveyard. The minister, Mr Thomson, bought Dunnikier House (now known as the Path House) from Mr Oswald in 1763, and leased from him a piece of the garden ground where the church was built in 1763. The church disappeared in 1901 when the new church was built at Dunnikier/Victoria Road.

Invertiel Parish Church. This church was built in 1837 and was sometimes known as Katie Shuttle's Church as it was within the sound of many weaving shuttles. Mr Stocks of the nearby linen works laid the foundation stone for the church that was sometimes earlier referred to as the Chapel of St Katherine. The building closed in 1952, with the congregation joining Invertiel Free Church, and was bought by Denis Harper, coachbuilder, whose business closed in Kirkcaldy in 1975. The church was demolished but the site is still undeveloped.

St James's Church, Port Brae. Originally St James was a Secession church which had met previously in Cowan Street in a building near the old Congregational Tabernacle. A church was built at the Port Brae in 1842 and closed in 1969, having rejoined the Church of Scotland. The building was closed as it was unsafe and there was no money for repairs. It was demolished in 1970 to make way for traffic lights and car parking. The last minister was the Rev. Williamson

St Peter's Episcopal Old Church, Townsend Place. After the 1745 Uprising, Episcopalianism was restricted to gatherings of no more than five, and it was some years before churches became established with encouragement from families like the Oswalds, Fergusons and Wemysses, who were becoming anglicized. The first church was built in 1811 on ground at the top of Coal Wynd and seated 122. It soon became too small and the next church was built in 1844 at Townsend Place. However, due to subsidence, it too was demolished and a new church was built on this site in 1976.

St John's Church, Meldrum Road. This Church of Scotland congregation opened in 1907, a foundation stone having been laid containing various papers in two glass bottles. When the church went on fire in 1975 these were retrieved. One wing of the church has remained as the church hall and a new church was built, the foundation stone being laid in 1976 with two glass bottles, one containing the contents of the 1907 bottles. The new church opened in 1977

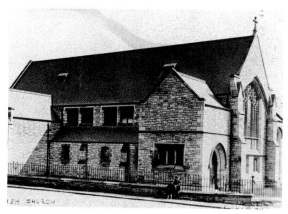

U. F. Church. Rosslyn Street. Gallatown.

Gallatown Free Church, Rossyln Street. This church started as a mission church from St Serfs, Dysart in 1857. The first church, built in 1877, became the church hall in 1884, then the Palladium Picture House and the Carpet Stores. Though that has now been demolished, the site still remains undeveloped. The main church, built in 1884, closed in 1977 when the congregation combined with Viewforth Parish Church to become Sinclairtown Church. The clock was donated by Mr Shepherd of Rossend Castle, Burntisland (Barry, Ostlere and Shepherd, Linoleum Manufacturers). The last minister was Rev. Fulton.

Loughborough Road Church. This church opened as a United Presbyterian church in 1881 and closed in 1969 after eighty-eight years of worship. In 1929 the congregation was reunited with the Church of Scotland. The building was demolished in 1985 and houses built on the site, although the church hall still remains and is used by the Brethren.

Right: Pathhead West, St Clair Street. In 1843 when the Disruption occurred, the congregation of the parish church split, and those against patronage left and set up a new congregation which became known as the East Free Church, later Pathhead West. It opened in a new building at the foot of St Clair Street in 1844, with seating for 700. In 1859 a gallery was built, increasing the seating to 830. John Buchan's father was minister from 1876 to 1888. Rev. Bernard Citron was the last minister. The congregation recombined with Pathhead East in 1958, becoming Pathhead Parish, with Rev. Citron as the first minister of the combined church. The old church was demolished in 1963 to make way for multi-storey flats.

Below: Free Church, Millie Street. The congregation broke away from the West Church in 1900 and this new building was opened in 1910. It was bought by Grubbs Car Sales and demolished around 1989. A new modern Free Church was built in St Clair Street, opening in 1992 with seating for 250 people. The manse is in St Mary's Road (from a painting by the late James Conway, session clerk).

Free Church, Tolbooth Street. At the time of the Disruption, the congregation walked out of St Brisse, the parish church, opening their new church in Tolbooth Street in 1844. A move was necessary because the premises were not big enough and a new church, St Brycedale's, opened in 1881 on land given by Provost Patrick Don Swan from the grounds of St Brycedale House (Hunter Hospital, now closed). St Brisse's then became known as the Old Kirk. The Tolbooth church eventually became the funeral premises of the Co-operative Society, most of which was demolished when Marks and Spencers expanded, except for a small gable with a memorial plaque.

Old Congregational Tabernacle, Cowan Street. The congregation set up around the end of the eighteenth century and in 1802 a church known as the 'Tabernacle' was built at the corner of Cowan and Charlotte Streets, seating 450 and costing £650. The fourth minister was Robert Aitkenhead who later sided with adult instead of infant baptism. However, the church worked surprisingly harmoniously with these different philosophies. In 1874 the West End Congregational Church opened on the High Street, replacing the Tabernacle.

Seven

Public Buildings

About 200 years ago there were few public buildings other than the churches that were then at the centre of the social life of the times. There were a few hotels or inns which were popular and some small inefficient hospitals. As the Industrial Revolution brought people into towns from the country areas, often to squalid living conditions, so public buildings appeared, including modern hospitals, halls, libraries, museums and cinemas.

The Tolbooth or Town House on the High Street was built in 1825, replacing an older building in Tolbooth Street. The High Street building was demolished in 1935 to make way for Marks and Spencer, and had a fine steeple with a clock, so Marks and Spencer placed a clock on their building. At the foot of Kirk Wynd was once the Mercat Cross and it was said of the town: 'Kirkcaldy pair people pulled down the Cross tae build the steeple.' The stone from the Mercat Cross was used to build the steeple of the old Tolbooth in 1782. Building of the present Town House commenced before the start of the Second World War and was completed post-war, partly opening in 1953 and fully in 1956. Tolbooths were also places where wrong-doers could be locked up.

Left: Dunnikier Town House was built in Commercial Street in what today is known as Pathhead. This was originally Dunnikier until the Oswalds built their new mansion house at Dunnikier in 1790. This town house opened in 1832 and was first used as a temporary hospital for cholera victims in what was the first outbreak of Asiatic cholera in the country. The building became surplus to requirements in 1876 when Pathhead became part of Kirkcaldy Burgh. It was demolished prior to 1907 when the Pathhead and Sinclairtown Reform Co-operative Society's new buildings were built on the site.

Below: Strathearn Paint Company, previously the Commercial Bank. This building on St Clair Street, opposite the entrance to Commercial Street, was originally built as a Commercial Bank and bank manager's house around 1890. At this time many industries were opening up in this part of Kirkcaldy followed by schools and banks. At the time of the photograph the words 'Commercial Bank' could be read on the inside glass of one of the windows. The bank closed and the Strathearn Paint Company took over. After 1985 it was used by various advisory bodies until, having been bought by the Council, it was demolished and the area landscaped in 1994.

Right: Kirkcaldy Abattoir. Kirkcaldy Abbatoir was built in 1933, replacing many smaller sub-standard slaughter houses. It was eventually closed in 1987 and demolished a few years later. The Royal Mail have now built their new premises on the site along with a number of other small units. The front brick wall has been listed and thus retained.

Below: Battery Place was a double-gable tenement building on the Esplanade on the other side of Glasswork Street from Volunteers' Green, seen here on the left. Originally built for families, the building later became the Booking Office for Alexander's buses until the new offices were built in 1961 at Invertiel. Thistle and Cowan Streets can be seen running from the centre to the right of the photograph. Volunteers' Green is here being used as a drying green.

Left: Old Trades Hall, Kirk Wynd, *c.*1880. The Poor House in Kirk Wynd, built in 1754, belonged to the Old Parish Church. Here twelve destitute people were looked after by the church but in return worked for their keep. The house was demolished in 1808, being too expensive to maintain, and new steps were built on the site from Kirk Wynd into the Kirkyard. In 1890 the Hendry Hall was built by Daniel Hendry, Linen and Linoleum Manufacturer on the site of the Old Trades Hall, then surplus to requirements.

Below: Fever Hospital and Sanatorium. Kirkcaldy's Fever Hospital was built on a site that was then outside Kirkcaldy in 1901 and the Sanatorium opened in 1910. The photograph shows one ward, the Sanatorium, for tuberculosis patients. The hospital consisted of a number of small single-storey wards around the nurses home, which is still there. Most, but not all, of the single-storey wards have been replaced. This hospital became the Victoria Hospital, at one time covering all but maternity and geriatric cases. The Surgical Block opened in 1961 and Tower Block in 1967. The old General Hospital in Nether Street closed shortly after this in 1970.

Sanitorium, Kirkcaldy

Right: Cottage Hospital, *c.*1895. The Cottage Hospital was originally gifted to the town of Kirkcaldy in 1889 by Michael Barker Nairn on grounds once part of his Dysart House. Michael Baker Nairn was given a baronetcy in 1904.

Below: Cottage Hospital with new round wards, *c.*1920. The hospital grew and new round wards were added in 1901. Michael Barker Nairn had seen these in the States and thought they would look attractive in Kirkcaldy. They were large round wards, each with about twenty beds. The hospital was closed in 1970, by which time it was the Orthopaedic Hospital, and demolished in 1986 when new private flats, the Kyles, were built on the site. The Kyles were named after the game often played here up until the end of the Second World War, 'Bawbee-She-Kyles'. It was played in Ravenscraig Castle and later on Dominic's Green in Ravenscraig Park. Sir Michael Barker Nairn, son of Sir Michael, gifted the park to the Burgh of Kirkcaldy in 1929, after which time his Kirkcaldy home, Dysart House, was sold. The hospital lintel stone, inscribed with '1889 I was sick and ye visited me', was saved and can be seen outside the Victoria Hospital, facing Hayfield Road.

Cottage Hospital, Kirkcaldy.

Kirkcaldy Museum and Art Gallery, 1925. The Museum and Art Gallery was gifted by John Nairn on the site of Balsusney House and opened in 1925 as part of the War Memorial in memory of the many men who died for their country, including his only son, Ian, killed at the end of the Great War. In 1928, Mr Nairn added the library, which includes the Beveridge Library from the Adam Smith Halls. Kirkcaldy Art Gallery is one of the finest in Scotland, with its Beveridge Library collection of MacTaggart and Peploe paintings. The tall buildings of Barry Ostlere and Shepherd can be seen on the far side of the railway line.

'Royal Burgh of Kirkcaldy, birthplace of Adam Smith'. In 1998 the sign was replaced with 'Welcome to Kirkcaldy, the Langtoun. Twin Town Ingolstadt'. Many visitors come every year to see what is left to link Kirkcaldy with Adam Smith. Ingolstadt is not one of the most important of European cities and is little known outside Kirkcaldy.

Above: Labour Exchange, *c*.1960. Kirkcaldy Labour Exchange, a red sandstone building, was on the Esplanade built after the Esplanade wall was completed in 1923. At times those working there were cut off by high spring tides and flooding. The building was demolished around 1979 to make way for the widening of the Esplanade, and a new Job Centre was built at the corner of Redburn Wynd and High Street in 1976. This has now moved on to a new building on the corner of Hunter Street.

Right: The Liberal Club, *c*.1914. The Liberal Club was on Oswald's Wynd and was obviously a busy social club in its time, particularly when the Liberal Government was in power. In 1908 when Herbert Asquith was Prime Minister, he came to Kirkcaldy, visiting the King's Theatre and the Liberal Club, and was made a Freeman of the Burgh. The Co-op was built on the corner of High Street and Oswald's Wynd in 1906 and expanded into the site occupied by the Liberal club, using the upper floors as a restaurant. When the Co-op burnt down in 1975, the Liberal Club building had to be demolished.

Left: The Kirkcaldy Corn Exchange. The Corn Exchange was opened in Market Street in 1859. This was the first real public hall in Kirkcaldy and was used for concerts, exhibitions and later for film shows when it was known as the Pavilion. The first silent 'movies' were seen in the Corn Exchange in 1894—moving shadows seen on a suspended wet cloth! The building was demolished in the early 1960s.

Below: Seafield Café. Seafield Café and Seafield Beach was once a favourite haunt of Kirkcaldy folk in the summer time. The Café was on the south side of Tiel Burn and was close to the site of the last bus garage, built in 1938. The other two garages had been built in 1930.

Eight

Transport

In sailing ship days, Kirkcaldy's harbour was very significant for international trade that included grain, and had many ferries to and from Edinburgh. Its bay is well sheltered from westerly winds, but exposed to the rarer easterly winds blowing up the Forth. Breakwaters were therefore built to the east, dividing the port from the mouth of the Den Burn, with a quay on its sheltered western side and a smaller pier to the south. Around 1800, the tiny harbour was congested with sailing vessels of all kinds, carrying coal, grain, linen and other cargoes, depicted in a contemporary painting looking north-eastwards towards Pathhead and Ravenscraig. Repeated improvements retained the pattern, and in 1847 the new railway brought a steep freight-only branch to the east quay–from this the sidings fanned out. Coal was still exported through these up until around 1972, while grain and scrap metal were handled for a few more years. The harbour has had no ships in over the last nine years and is now effectively closed.

Nineteenth-century view of Kirkcaldy Harbour.

Mid-nineteenth-century view of Kirkcaldy Harbour. The buildings on the left were replaced by Nairn's Canvas factory in 1868 and added to in 1914. Some of the ancient stonework of the quay on the right can still be seen amid the early twentieth-century concrete at the foot of Robert Hutchison's grain silo.

Loading linoleum onto ships. This tall ship's funnel and complete lack of motor vehicles suggest that this view dates from around 1910; the original caption stated 'loading bales of linoleum' but this local product was, of course, always rolled.

Around 1960, various ships, including the MV *British Coast* (seen here alongside the High Street quay), were employed in the floor coverings trade. Rolls of linoleum and packs of vinyl floor tiles were carried to London where some were shipped overseas.

Kirkcaldy Harbour. Nairn's Canvas factory features largely in this view taken in the 1950s of the ship that brought in cork from Portugal for linoleum factories. As lorries and ships grew larger, and coal waste was tipped on the coast at Dysart, the port became uneconomic to dredge. The branch railway line was abandoned and today under privatised Forth Ports, no ships call here.

Left: Kirkcaldy's first passenger station, 1910. Kirkcaldy's first passenger station building was opened in 1847 on the west side of the town, and has since been twice replaced. Here, a steam train is seen leaving the station in 1910, as a mother and daughter await the arrival of their own train. The growth of passenger traffic saw the reconstruction of the station in 1965 and the loss of its extensive canopies. On the left the linoleum works of Barry, Ostlere and Shepherd can be seen. The smell of the works led to an association with Kirkcaldy—to put it in the words of the poem by Mary Campbell Smith from the *Boy on the Train*: 'For I ken mysel' by the queer-like smell, that the next stop's Kirkcaddy'. The smell still occurs, but only occasionally now.

Below: Nicol Street arch bridge, 1847–1997. The Edinburgh and Northern Railway opened in September 1847, connecting Kirkcaldy with the national network. However, it was not until the Forth Rail Bridge opened in 1890 that a direct rail route between Edinburgh and Aberdeen was opened, and the ferries across the Forth and Tay were stopped. This stone arch bridge in Nicol Street carried main line trains for nearly 150 years, despite its restricted clearance of less than fifteen feet, and settlement due to mine workings. It was demolished in February 1997 and replaced by a modern bridge on the original abutments.

Right: Kirkcaldy Goods Yard with a steam engine. The large timber goods shed on the left was used to transfer linoleum from road to rail and later became a free car park. To the right stood Barry, Ostlere and Shepherd's linoleum factories, now the site of the College of Nursing. North of the down platform stood the Kirkcaldy Signal Box, demolished

around 1980; now local signals and points are controlled remotely from the Edinburgh Signalling Centre. Rail freight dwindled after 1953 and the final traffic through this yard, fertilisers, ended in the 1980s.

Below: Diesel railcars introduced under the British Railway 1955 Plan. The railcar seen on the up platform on 6 February 1988 was a refugee from the re-opened Bathgate line. To the right is the canopy of the main 1960s station building, which burned out later in 1988 and was again replaced in 1991. Now Kirkcaldy has several daily through-trains to London and has a faster and more frequent train service to Edinburgh, Dundee, Aberdeen, Inverness and local stations, than ever before, including the circle line via Thornton, Cowdenbeath and Dunfermline.

Above: Sinclairtown Railway Station was opened in 1847. This photograph shows the original site facing the St Clair Street overbridge. In order to improve goods facilities, the passenger station was moved northwards into the cutting beyond the bridge, which was widened on the east side to provide a forecourt and station building above the tracks before the station entrance. The station closed to passengers in 1969 and to goods in 1970.

Left: An Albion bus, c.1930. This is an early view of a bus driver with his 'clippie'. The last clippies finished work in 1981, by which time driver-only buses were introduced with 'exact fares'.

High Street at the foot of Coal Wynd. This part of High Street, if not suffering from burst water mains, was often flooded from the distant Pannie Pit at Smeaton Road, which was part of the Dunnikier Colliery that closed in 1926 after the General Strike, abandoned in 1927 and demolished in 1931–1932. Here, anxious passengers leave the tramcar, whose further progress seems doubtful.

Tramcar terminus at 'Top o' the Town' Gallatown. The original 1903 municipal electric tramway terminus at Gallatown was this loop in Rosslyn Street near the Oswald Road car sheds. In 1906, its 107cm (3' 6") gauge track was extended to Leven by the Wemyss & District Tramway Company, and until 1931 some services ran right through between Leven and Linktown. The Wemyss Company outlasted the corporation tramways by a year

Left: Coming down Kirk Wynd. The new electric lamp column illustrates that this view of Kirk Wynd dates from soon after the Victoria Power Station opened in 1903. Not long before this, in 1890, the Hendry Hall had replaced the Old Trades Hall alongside the church steps. On the left the very plain premises of the Fife Free Press now occupies the site of the engineer's attractively pantiled house and shop.

Below: Large and small horse-drawn transport. The pony cart shows that some local cartage jobs were very small in the 1930s. Ahead, the great carthorse is controlling the dray laden with rolls of linoleum as it trundles down the steep Path to the harbour. On the right are the roof vents of the Holmes maltings, finally demolished in 1997, and to the rear are some of Nairn's early buildings.

Above: Pneumatic tyres show that this was one of the last horsedrawn Co-operative vans, on display at the Basin soon after completion of the Esplanade in 1923. It was probably given its distinctive finish by a local coachbuilder, very likely Ronaldson.

Below: Despite its ominous number, this pristine Co-operative van was proudly on display at the Basin around 1930—the similarity of finish with the vehicle above suggests that the same coach painter was responsible.

Tramcar Terminus, Oswald Road. After the corporation tramcars stopped running in 1931, the tram shed at Oswald Road became a repair workshop for Walter Alexander, who ran replacement bus services on behalf of the Town Council. In later years, when all bus repair work had been taken to the Esplanade garage, the building was used by local haulier and scrap merchant Thomas Muir. The pink sandstone edifice was demolished around 1990.

These bowler-hatted gentlemen are in celebratory mood. This was the 1903 opening of the Kirkcaldy tramways.

A charabanc outing, c.1922. A fully laden charabanc of Stoddart's General Motor Carrying Company stands ready to go outside the early-nineteenth-century offices of Innes the solicitors at 199 High Street. Passengers entered through separate nearside doors, their shapes echoed in the offside coachwork. Its solid tyres no doubt caused bruising by which they would remember the trip for days to come.

Forty years later, buses were much more sophisticated. Here, Walter Alexander's foreman coachbuilder Gordon Reid displays a new 1959 bus alongside a much older model outside the Oswald Road repair workshop.

The late-1920s lorry with its milk churns standing near the foot of Coal Wynd is adding to the traffic problems caused by burst water mains, which had loosened the granite setts in the High Street.

This was evidently the latest thing in tipper lorries around the time of the Second World War, but by 1977 no contractor of this name was listed for Kirkcaldy

Coal Wynd, c.1965. This cleared area of ground between Coal Wynd and Stewart's Lane proved handy for parking the vans which distributed the products of Beattie's Bakery. Until 1985 this was situated in what had once been a jam factory. Originally a mill, it was rebuilt in Coal Wynd after a fire by the Swan brothers. It houses a number of small business units today.

Kirkcaldy High Street, c.1960. This shows the High Street before one-way traffic was introduced. The High Street was pedestrianized in 1981.

The country bus station was sited on the Esplanade in the 1930s and the shelters were built in 1951. This site was naively chosen to suit day-trippers to the still-popular local beaches and soon became untenable due to glass-smashing waves and repeated sea flooding caused by high spring tides and strong easterly winds. Tipping of coal waste at Dysart blackened Kirkcaldy's strand, and warmer beaches became more accessible. The country bus station was abandoned in 1983 when the town bus station was extended to accommodate all services.

In 1948 Andrew Thomson of Coaltown of Balgonie founded a mobile greengrocery business in Invertiel Terrace. It was later based at Riley's market garden, now covered by the workshops of Fife Scottish Buses. In 1952 his brother Robert left the army and joined the business, and for twenty-five years they both sold vegetables around the town from horse-drawn carts. Andrew died in 1977, but Robert still carried on with Billy, Kirkcaldy's last working horse. Billy retired in 1988 and the cart has now been replaced with a small motor van

Nine

Industry

Much of the early industry in Kirkcaldy centred around the home and was comprised mainly of weaving and nail making, or along the coast with salt pans. With the Industrial Revolution, factories were built, and the change from water power to steam power led to the development of coal mines. Linen was one of the main manufactured products, together with sail cloth, but as sailing ships were being replaced with steamships, people like Michael Nairn looked for some other associated product. He came up with floorcloth and built his factory in Pathhead in 1847, with the name 'linoleum' being universally adopted later. Kirkcaldy also had heavy engineering and manufactured such as rice crushing machinery. Douglas and Grant had started making guns for the Crimean War (1856–1858), while furniture was made for the growing middle classes. The railway came to Kirkcaldy in 1847, and both the harbour and the rail network were used to bring raw materials in and take manufactured items out.

Kirkcaldy Harbour, c.1850. Customs officials stand on pitch (a by-product of the Kirkcaldy Gas Works), waiting to be filled into barrels. On the foreshore are Ravenscraig Chemical Works and the Whale Oil boiling shed. On the skyline is M. Nairn & Co.'s Floorcloth Works, 'Nairn's Folly', built in 1847 and demolished in May 1967 to make way for widening in Nether Street, and Ravenscraig Castle, built for James II in 1460. The Castle is one of the few old buildings in Kirkcaldy that is still standing.

Left: Whaler *Lord Gambiar*, owned by Swan Bros, in Kirkcaldy Harbour, c.1860. Built in Sunderland in 1825, she, along with two other ships, were lost in the Arctic in 1862. Fortunately, the crew were taken in by local Inuits and rescued four months later. Kirkcaldy's last whaler was sold in 1866.

Below: Nairn's Canvas Factory, with its entrance in Hill Place, was built in 1828 by Michael Nairn at the top of his garden. His house was part of today's Port Brae Bar. After use as a canvas factory, this building became the Travel Club, and was later demolished to make way for two houses.

Right: This photograph, taken around 1900, shows the 'Auld Bucket Pats', a favourite place for paddling at low tide, now unfortunately buried under the Promenade. These man-made depressions in the rock, to retain the seawater, were all that remained of a once-thriving salt industry—salt had been produced in Kirkcaldy since at least the sixteenth century by evaporating seawater over a coal fire until only salt remained. Purer imports from Holland led to the demise of this old industry by the mid-nineteenth-century.

Below: Reilly's Salt Works was situated on Sands Road before the Esplanade was built. The works refined salt from rock salt. In earlier times there had been salt pans on the shore owned by Oswald's of Dunnikier, but high salt taxes and more modern methods of production had made this method more cost effective. Reilly also had a branch in Leven.

Link's Pottery, situated in Pottery Wynd (now named Methven Street) off Links Street, had its origins in 1714 when William Adam (father of Robert Adam) contracted to the owners of Raith Estate to dig clay from the fields which are now Balwerie School playing fields. Over the next 214 years, various pottery works were on this site, under several owners (mainly the Methven family). The last pottery here closed in 1928.

Fife Pottery stood at the corner of Rosslyn Street and Pottery Street, Gallatown. It was built by brothers Andrew and Archibald Grey in 1817. On their bankruptcy in 1826, the works was bought by John Methven, owner of Links Pottery, and on his death in 1837, Fife Pottery was passed to his daughter and son-in-law, Mary and Robert Methven Heron. Their son Robert introduced Weymss Ware around 1880–1882. Designer Karel Nekola, recruited from Germany, did much of the famous art work.

Barry, Ostlere and Shepherd's main building stood at the north side of the railway station in Forth Avenue. The area is now landscaped. Barry and Ostlere set up a linoleum business in 1881, having previously been employed by Shepherd and Beveridge. After the death of Provost Michael Beveridge, Shepherd joined them in 1899. Buying up old and dying buildings, the firm expanded to having at least twelve factories in Kirkcaldy. The firm closed due to competition in 1964. Note the advertisement for the Co-op on the hoarding on the south side of the railway line, and the nose of a steam train at the station.

The inspection and packaging line in Smeaton Warehouse of Nairn's tile factory, c.1958. This new warehouse was started in 1955 and today forms part of the complex on the south side of Den Road. Nairn's linoleum tiles were the first DIY flooring tiles. Note the girls wearing headscarves covering their rollers—'Big night out tonight!'

Above: Caledonian Mill, Prime Gilt Box Street. James Meikle started up a carpet factory in Dysart in 1919 and in 1956 expanded, moving the carpet weaving part of the Works into the now vacant Caledonian Mill in Prime Gilt Box Street. The works had been built in 1898 when Robert Weymss moved his linen works from Abbotshall Mill, which exited through the Weymss Buildings onto the High Street. Robert Weymss closed his works and, sadly, Meikles closed in 1980. It had been hoped that the buildings would become a warehouse, but they were demolished and houses built on the site in 1988.

Below: Lockhart's Links Linen Factory. Ninian Lockhart came to Kirkcaldy from Newburgh in 1797 and set up a small weaving business in Linktown. He would rise early in the

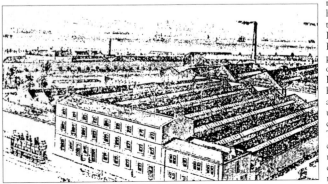

morning and take his linen on foot to markets in Dundee and Perth. His family business prospered, and, on the site on Burleigh Street, his factory grew and grew until unfortunately it closed in 1981. The buildings were demolished and retail outlets were constructed in their place.

Above: Bennochy Works. Bennochy Works were built in 1864 by Ninian Lockhart, eldest son of Ninian Lockhart of the Links, who in 1850 established a separate spinning business from his father. This was a very successful business and continued until its closure in 1984. The building, typical of the tall late-nineteenth-century factory buildings, was sadly demolished in 1985 to make way for new flats at 'Abbotsmill'. The four-storey building was well built with a solid iron frame and a tall chimney. It was a pity, however, that the mill could not have been converted to some other use, as has been successfully seen with the Foyer, from the old West Spinning Mill. Ninian Lockhart Jr was a lay preacher of the Scottish Baptist Church in Rose Street, and his son William Peddie moved to the Midlands where he was also a well-known preacher. Ninian Lockhart Jr died in the Whyte House in Kirkcaldy in 1880.

Right: Inside the Bennochy works, 1985.

Kirkcaldy

Hutchison's Maltings. In 1825, Robert Hutchison established a corn shop in the High Street and later bought a milling business at East Bridge in 1854 and the house, which is now a listed building, on the Path. Here, he developed a flour mill and a maltings (the Maltings were demolished in 1997). The old maltings' hoppers were said to have golden cockerels on the apex of the roof. It is not easy to see from this old photograph. In 1870 the maltings and mill were thought to have been the largest in Scotland. Hutchison's railway sidings connected with the main railway and the harbour and brought in much grain, imported from other parts of the country and from Europe. The milling side of the business still thrives at the harbour.

Harbour Warehouse. This little building, sited between the silos and the inner dock, was for storing grain that was brought in off ships in the harbour. Sadly, it was never listed and disappeared around 1984 to make room for large lorry tankers.

McIntosh Furniture Factory, Victoria Road, *c.*1930. Alexander Henry McIntosh came to Kirkcaldy to work for Samuel Barnet, joiner, in the Linktown when he was nineteen. He worked for fifteen years with Samuel Barnet and his son before setting up his own business in 1869. Alexander was very successful and in 1880 built his typical late-nineteenth-century four-storey factory building with a railway siding, on Victoria Road. Many people thought that he was too far out of town to be successful, but a few years later he took over the defunct John Keys boiler making site alongside. The business thrived after the First and Second World Wars, and was also involved in fitting out the *Queen Mary* and the *Queen Elizabeth*. In 1970 the business moved to a modern, purpose-built factory, all on one level at Mitchelston Industrial Estate. Railway links were no longer needed and all transport was by road.

War work at McIntosh's Factory. During the war years the factory was engaged in making wings and other parts for aeroplanes. In this photograph wings are being manufactured for First World War aircrafts.

Invertiel Rope Works. Rope works were established here by Thomas Renton in 1843, and the 400 metre rope walk was built on the site of an earlier rope works in 1850. It was here that long marine cables for ships like the *Queen Mary* were made. Hendry's West Spinning Mill became part of the business, making post office twine, which has now been replaced with rubber bands. The business closed in 1973 and the Rope Walk was demolished in 1987.

The Lido Outdoor Seawater Bathing Pool, later Alma Confectionery. The Lido fresh water swimming pool was built at Seafield in 1936 on the site of the old Chemical Works (see p.51). It closed during the war years, but swimming continued after the war ended, until 1953. It was then bought by the Alma Confectionery, who made popular children's sweets like 'skull crushers'. The business eventually moved to Dundee in 1991 before finally closing in 1993. The Lido building caught fire in 1994 and what remained was demolished.

Seafield Colliery. The first sod of the Seafield Colliery was cut in 1954 and the colliery was closed after an underground fire in 1988. The towers were demolished in 1989 and houses have now been built on the site. Seafield ran underground trains to the coal face and at one time employed over 2,000 miners, with workings extended under the sea and connected with both the Michael and the Frances collieries. There was no spoil as all waste was disposed of underground. The twin towers encased the mine wheels.

Denis Harper's Coachbuilding Works. Denis Harper started his first coach building and repair works in Thistle Street in 1947. When Invertiel Parish Church closed in 1952, he bought the church, had it deconsecrated and expanded his business there. The area in the foreground became an automatic car wash. He closed his works in Kirkcaldy in 1975, continuing the business in Edinburgh. The church was demolished shortly after this, and the area is still undeveloped.

John Leitch Foundry, Katherine Street. This building was completed in 1921, when John Leitch established his 'ferrous and non-ferrous' castings company. Manhole or service covers can still be seen in the streets of Kirkcaldy with the name John Leitch. The business closed around 1985 and Bordax moved in and continued with a welding business. The firm moved to Glenrothes in 1985 where they are no longer involved in manufacture, and the building was demolished along with the Meikles factory to make way for housing. This ground is still undeveloped.

Old Gas Tank, Links. The Gas Works was established in the Links in 1834. It expanded in 1876, leading to a court action as the Council had acquired a part of Volunteers' Green, a public drying green, for a gas works and midden. The court case was lost but in order to prevent the demolition of new buildings the Council gave an exchange piece of ground to the people. This was 'Fraser's Green' in Nicol Street, about quarter of a mile away. North Sea gas made the manufacture of town gas unnecessary and the buildings have been demolished, the gas tank disappearing in 1981.

Ten

Events

Some events happen annually such as markets, galas and pageants. Other events are to mark certain occasions like the end of the First World War or the success of a team, while others are unplanned such as the beaching of a whale or sea floods.

High seas, c.1970, with the country station in the background and problems for motorists. Since the Esplanade was built in 1922–1923, there have been times when there are spring tides, south winds and a full moon when high seas have flooded the Esplanade right up to the High Street. At these times the Esplanade and associated parking is closed to motor vehicles, while in the past the country bus station (now moved) and people living on the front were often flooded. Sand bags and other barricades are used to prevent saltwater seeping in. Prior to the sea wall being built, the tide washed onto Sands Road and would often have entered gardens which ran along strips from the High Street houses. Attempts have been made to smarten up the Esplanade, but many plants will not tolerate too much salt spray and the plants need to be selected to withstand a salty atmosphere. The sea wall itself has become very unsightly, but there would be formidable damage if it was ever breached. There is still flooding in the area.

Above: Elephant Parade in the High Street, 1902. The Tolbooth and Town House in the High Street provided a great vantage point for parades. A circus coming to town would advertise its arrival by a parade of elephants and other animals, as did the internationally famous Barnum and Bailley's Circus in 1902.

Left: Military Parade in the High Street, 1905. Military parades also often took place along the High Street, which in earlier times was the town centre, with the Tolbooth there until 1935. Taking the salute at this 1905 parade, a review of the Artillery Volunteers, was General French, a Boer War General who visited Kirkcaldy in order to open up a practise range at Earlseat, five miles west of the town. The Volunteers were on parade in full dress uniform, not their battle dress.

Above: Celebrating the victory at Mafeking, Kirkcaldy High Street, 1900. The Boer War in South Africa began in 1899, with Kirkcaldy men numbering among its casualties. Thus, there was great rejoicing when Mafeking was relieved after a long siege by the Boers in February 1900.

Right: Bicycle Parade through the High Street, 1900. This photograph is believed to portray a bicycle parade through the High Street, but it appears that a number of carriages and carts were involved and that the bicycles did not have the field to themselves. Note the Barnet and Morton building, still in the High Street but now no longer an ironmonger, and the cobbles.

Above: Hurricane of 1968. On the night of 14 January 1948, a hurricane hit Scotland, causing severe damage to roofs, outbuildings and chimney pots. That night, part of the roof blew off the chair shop of A.H. McIntosh's furniture factory in Victoria Road. Photographs were taken of the damage and workers volunteered to repair this without a long wait for insurance estimates. Work in the factory was resumed within three weeks—quite a record! Many Kirkcaldy folk had worked all their lives there, and in some cases three generations in one family.

Below: Beached Whale, 1904. In 1904 this whale was washed up on the beach in Kirkcaldy and was bought for £2 by the owner of a manure factory in Dunfermline. After removing the flesh, the carcass was buried to allow it to clean, and then donated to Edinburgh University.

Right: Links Market, *c.*1920. The Links Market has been a feature of Linktown since 1304. Linktown was a separate Burgh from Kirkcaldy until 1876, which meant that goods could not be sold in Kirkcaldy without payment of dues to the Council, and therefore the Links had their own markets. Earlier markets were mainly for buying and selling, while today the Links Market is almost entirely for pleasure. On the third weekend in April it has been tradition for all the showground people in Scotland and the North of England to meet for five days in Kirkcaldy

where there is a mile long pleasure ground along the Esplanade. Originally, this was in Links Street, but the arrival of tramcars in 1903 meant the market moved to the Esplanade, whose closure still causes much traffic chaos today. The type of shows have changed over the years, the 'Wall of Death' is now never seen, nor the 'Tiny Lady!'

Below: Links Market, *c.*1960.

Left: The Pageant. Hospital pageants were started in 1923 in order to raise money for hospitals, and continued until 1948 and the emergence of the National Health Service. The pageant, however, started up again in 1951, this time to provide TV sets for hospitals and houses for disabled persons and pensioners. In 1968 the 'Lad and Lass' concept was introduced (replacing the 'Warden and Lass'), and the event became known as the Kirkcaldy Karnival. Lack of support led to the demise of the pageant, the last one being staged in 1977.

Below: The Pageant Float and Red Cross girls. Many floats were entered, and runners alongside these floats shook cans and buckets for contributions. Latterly, the centre piece to the parade, which usually travelled from the ice rink down to the town centre, was the carriage with the 'Langtoun Lad and Lass', who were the most important people of the day. They were carefully chosen by a committee for their public spiritedness. A lot of money was collected for the hospitals in this way, and in this photograph are a group of Red Cross girls 'doing their bit' for the good cause. Standing are, from left to right, Marion Renton, Ena Lawrie, Ann Todd and Ina Haig.

Right: Dunnikier Scouts and Cubs, 1954. The 17th Fife (Dunnikier Group) Scouts at the Rally of Cubs and Scouts at Raith Estate on the occasion of a visit by Chief Scout Lord Rowallen on 13 June 1954. Among those pictured are: Mr Ronaldson, Eddy McMahon, Dunc Yule, Archie Cook, Mike Dempsey, Bob Clark, Jack Morgan, Jimmy Reid, Mr Leslie, Andy Reid,

Menzies Morris, Les Stewart, Harry McMahon, Ronnie Hynd, Francis Dempsey, George Harvey, Bob Dick, Alec Yule, Mike Davie, Jim Wilson and Dave Brown.

Below: Almond Place, 1955. Before the time when every household owned a camera it was a great occasion when the street photographer paid a visit. The bairns of Almond Place pose for the camera with their favourite toys. From left to right, back row: Eddy Kelly, Ann Aitken, Catherine Clark, Jane Smith, Billy Fleming, David Purdy, Peter Christie, Alistair Malcolm, Brian Biglin, Margaret Aitkin, Jannette Stewart, James Monahen. Middle row: Mary Biglin, -?, Roy Smith, Brenda Robertson, Norma Grubb, Elinor McCauly, Elinor McDonald. Front row: Brian Aitkin, Billy Biglin, Jean Biglin, Freddie McDonald.

Left: The Royal Visit, 28 June 1948. King George VI and Queen Elizabeth arrived at Kirkcaldy Station at 11 a.m. and were met by Lord Elgin. Outside the library, they met many of the local dignitaries. Children were not given the day off school but were given time off to line the route and wave. The Royal couple left from Sinclairtown Station and were said to be delighted with their visit. The building in the centre is No.16, Weymyssfield, now a list B building.

Below: Seafield Gala, 1909. Most of the old terraced houses in this area have disappeared, including Horse Wynd, but at one time there was a little community nearby the Seafield Sands and Beach Café. In the background of the photograph is a chimney, probably of the Tyrie Linen Works, where many people in this area worked.

Eleven

Dysart

An independent Royal Burgh of long standing, Dysart was incorporated into the Burgh of Kirlcaldy in 1930. Many overtures had been made in the previous fifty years by Kirkcaldy for this to happen, but it was not until the demise of coal shipments from Dysart Harbour, owned by the town and its main source of revenue, that the inevitable merger happened. Separated physically from Kirkcaldy by the extensive grounds of Ravenscraig Park to the south, and the main west coast rail line to the west, Dysart retained its individual character and did not change much until the late 1950s, when, like most other places, it was the victim of a wholesale clearance of most of the oldest houses in the town. This was done with the best of motives as many of the dwellings were sub-standard, and indeed, hovels by today's standards. What these houses were replaced by and the change it made to the streetscape can be seen today, although with hindsight more could have been done to retain the unique atmosphere so well remembered by its older inhabitants. Of the once flourishing coal industry, there remains only the gaunt skeleton of the Frances Colliery's head gear to remind one of the main source of employment, the three Dysart pits. The Frances closed in 1985 after the disastrous year-long strike. The Randolph had closed in 1968, while the Lady Blanche's closure in 1929 had sealed the fate of Dysart as a coal shipping port. The working of coal seams near to the surface is recorded as early as the thirteenth century and its availability was instrumental in making another early industry, salt manufacture, so successful that Dysart was known as the 'Salt Burgh'. In the seventeenth century Dysart was also called 'Little Holland' due to its extensive trade with the Low Countries. The spinning of flax and the weaving of linen was well established in the middle of the eighteenth century and reached its peak in the mills of Normand, Harrow, Terrace and Smith, from the mid-1800s to the First World War. Shipbuilding carried on at the harbour from 1764 to 1880, steel ships eventually making obsolete the wooden type built with great skill by the Dysart shipwrights.

DYSART FROM THE PIER

Dysart from the shore,
c.1900.

Left: Pan Ha, c.1890. The large chimney and winding gear of the Lady Blanche colliery sit above the picturesque sixteenth and seventeenth-century houses where many of the miners lived. Sunk in 1875, the Lady Blanche was the successor to an earlier coal mine called the Engine Pit, which was a short distance to the east. This pit, opened in 1754, was one of the first in Scotland to use a steam engine to pump water from the workings. The total cost of sinking the shaft, and engine and boiler was £377 9s 10d. The Lady Blanche closed in 1929.

Below: Workers at the Lady Blanche pithead, c.1912. The women in the middle of this photograph worked at the pithead sorting waste from the coal. The employment of women underground was outlawed in 1842.

Right: Frances Colliery, *c*.1920. Originally called Dysart Colliery, work began on the shaft in 1850. Owned by the Earl of Rosslyn's coal company, as were Randolph and Lady Blanche, it was to become the oldest producing deep mine in Scotland. The coal washer was installed in 1905 and the bulk of its output was transported by rail. Known locally as the Dubbie Pit, after the Dubbie Braes above

which it stood, it was ultimately to destroy this once popular beauty spot.

Below: Frances Colliery pithead, 1980. Within five years of this photograph being taken, coal mining in Dysart came to an end. A disastrous underground fire broke out during the year-long miners' strike, and in February 1985 the pit was closed with the loss of 500 jobs. It was kept mothballed for ten years, raising hopes that it would be reopened, but it was allowed to flood and the pithead buildings were demolished between 1994 and 1996. All that remains is the skeleton of the head frame erected in 1946.

Frances Colliery bing, 1960. Forty years of tipping at the Dubbie Braes produced a mountain of black waste which, spread by the sea, blighted the once golden beaches of Dysart and Kirkcaldy. The bing burnt for many years due to spontaneous combustion of the coal amongst the waste. In 1967 the National Coal Board applied for permission to tip westwards along the beach. Permission was duly granted and millions of tons of waste were dumped over the next fifteen years.

Sea coal gatherers, c.1956. A small scale industry which flourished for many years and was probably unique to Fife. The large percentage of coal contained in the waste which was tipped into the sea at the Frances, meant it was profitable to 'harvest this'. There was a ready market for this sea coal, and a horse and cart and wire-mesh scoops were all that were required to set up in business.

Dysart Harbour, c.1900. With eight ships in the dock and four in the outer harbour, this busy scene was typical up until the outbreak of the First World War. The majority of the ships using the harbour at this time were small wooden vessels, mostly Scandanavian, with a carrying capacity of three hundred tons.

The steamship SS *Turquoise* of Glasgow. This ship berthed in the dock in October 1901. At one hundred and sixty-five feet, it was the largest steamer at that time to enter harbour, and she loaded six hundred tons of coal. One of the steel chutes used to load the coal into the ships can be seen suspended from the pier.

SS *Topaz* of Glasgow, sister ship to the *Turquoise*. She entered the dock in February 1905 and loaded seven hundred tons of coal. The press report stated that 'three Norwegian steamers, each of about five hundred tons are expected shortly'. The days of the wooden sailing ships were coming to an end.

Ship under construction, c.1880. This view of the harbour is one of the few to show a ship under construction at the shipyard. Shipbuilding began around 1760, and flourished until 1882 when the move to iron and steel ships caused the collapse of the wooden ship building industry. The shipyard remained in use until the end of the century, under several owners who built small fishing boats and carried out repair work.

Above and below: Although he was not native to Dysart, James MacLeod was destined to hold the highest office the town could bestow. Elected to the Town Council in 1902, he was made Baillie in 1909 and attained the position of Provost in 1919. He served in this capacity until the amalgamation with Kirkcaldy in 1930, the last of a long line of distinguished men who served Dysart so well over the centuries. *Above*: James MacLeod opens his saddler and harness maker business in Townhead, Dysart. *Below left*: The business is transferred to new premises in Normand Road, Dysart. *Below right*: Mr MacLeod stands proudly in his role as Provost.

Robert Gordon's hairdressers shop, 65 High Street, July 1904. The business was bought from Mr A.M. Reid for £20 and included stock, fittings and furniture. From left to right are: John Gordon, the owner Robert Gordon, who had to sell up in November 1916 when he was called up for service in the First World War, and his father David Gordon.

Fowler's newsagents, 61 High Street, c.1915. There were two newsagents in Dysart for many years; this one, Fowler, and at the Cross, Owler, which must have caused some confusion! Robert Fowler, on the extreme left beside his father, carried on the business well into the 1960s.

Dysart Co-operative, Normand Road, c.1947. Built in the 1930s to serve the housing developments of Bellfield Crescent, Cook Street and Stewart Street, it contained baker, butcher and grocery departments.

Jimmy Lawrie and his horse Donald, c.1960. Mr Lawrie was the last of the Co-op roundsmen to use horse-drawn transport. The stables in Anderson Street were then used as garages for motor transport. This photograph was taken outside the Co-operative Dairy in Anderson Street. Just visible on the extreme left is the barrow of John McLean, for many years a street sweeper in Dysart. By way of typical Dysart humour, a riddle was often posed– 'What goes up the road and doon the road but never touches the road? Answer–Jock McLean!'

The Model T Ford delivery van of Alexander Clark, *c.*1920. Dysart had three dairies at the beginning of the twentieth century.

Ice cream barrow, *c.*1925. George Cascarino with his ice cream barrow at the Back o' the Ashlar.

High Street looking west, c.1905. The buildings on the right were the premises of Dysart Co-operative Society, founded in 1846. Every need could be catered for by the 'Store' as it was known locally, and when the last of the shops, the grocery department, closed in 1988, it was a sad day for Dysart.

The Cross looking east, c.1947. The Cross was once the market place of Dysart and fortunately has retained many of its finest buildings. The Tolbooth, which was built in 1576, and the Town Hall, built in 1887, are listed buildings, and the seventeenth and eighteenth- century houses on the left were demolished and rebuilt exactly as they were. The lamp was erected in 1887 to commemorate the golden jubilee of Queen Victoria.

Dysart Station, c.1904. No trace of the station buildings remain today, only the names Station Road and Station Court, a new housing development, exist as reminders of a service that started in 1847. The station closed in 1968 as part of the Beeching cuts, but at present there are plans to build a station to serve Kirkcaldy east, and Dysart appears to be a favoured site.

Station staff, c.1912. On the right is one of the policemen from Dysart's force of an inspector and two constables who were stationed at Victoria Street

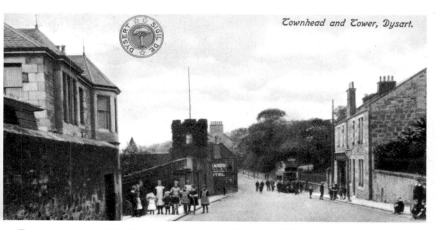

Tramway terminus, 1915. The tram service came to Dysart in 1911, eight years after the Kirkcaldy system started. Provost Anderson, a full compliment of baillies and councillors, and a large crowd gathered to witness the great event.

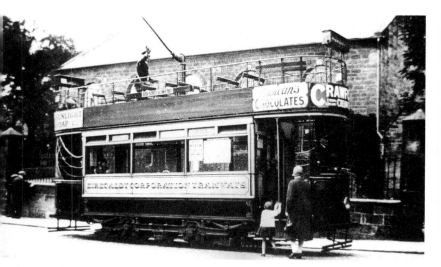

A tram at the terminus outside the Barony church, c.1930. The tram service was to last only a year after this photograph was taken. Competition from bus operators led to the demise of the trams and the last runs were made on 15 May 1931. The tram rails lay on the roads until the Second World War, when they were lifted to be used in the coal mines as girders, steel being short in supply.

Back of Ashlar, c.1924. The Ashlar, or as it is called in Dysart, the Aisler, lies to the west of the harbour. The name comes from the French *aiseler*, a squared stone used in building. The cliff above the harbour still bears the marks of the quarriers' tools, where the stone was wrought for hundreds of years and used by French stone masons to build St Serf's Tower in the sixteenth century.

Beach in front of Piper's Braes, c.1924. The beach in front of the Pipers' Braes with its once golden sands. On the skyline can be seen the chimney and headgear of the Frances Colliery and the bing at the Dubbie Braes is beginning to spread out nearer the sea.

Dubbie Braes, c.1902. For many years a popular gathering for locals and the many visitors who came to Dysart on holiday. A natural spring rose at the foot of the Braes forming a large pond or 'dub', which gave the Braes their name. This pond was drained in 1894 and a bandstand was built on the site in 1897 as part of the improvements carried out for Queen Victoria's Diamond Jubilee celebrations. The local militia, No. 9 (Dysart) Company, Fife Volunteer Artillery, had two cannons and a rifle range there. These were removed in 1905 and a café was built on the site of the ammunition magazine. The café burnt down in 1931.

The Man in the Rock, c.1905. This figure, carved in relief at the Red Rocks to the east of the Dubbie Braes, was made by John Patterson, a Dysart handloom weaver, in 1851. It represented Bonivard in Byron's poem *The Prisoner of Chillon*. The wall at the base of the sculpture and the railing were paid for by public subscription, and it became a well-known and much-visited landmark. The cliff face it was carved on eventually became undermined by the sea, collapsing during a violent easterly storm in 1970.

Above: Launching of the *Endeavour*, built in 1946 by Will Carr.

Left: *Firefly*, built by Tom Carrington, 1953. The Dysart yawl was seventeen feet long and, carrying a dipping-lug sail of impressive proportions, was a familiar sight on the Forth for over a century. This refined version of the 'Fifie' fishing boat was built mainly by coal miners and raced in regattas on the Fife coast. Competition between Dysart and West Wemyss crews was especially fierce. Silting up of the small harbours, caused by colliery waste being dumped into the sea from the Frances and Michael pits, brought the regattas to an end in the mid-1950s.

Opposite above: Crowning of the Dysart Queen, 1953. This annual event was organised by the Dysart Hospital Pageant Committee and was held in Ravenscraig Park. There were games for the children, dancing and a fireworks display. Money raised on the day was donated to the Cottage Hospital. The Queen in this instance was Miss Mary Bald, and she was crowned by Miss Janet Meikle. In the 1930s the Earl and Countess of Rosslyn and the writer Annie S. Swan were amongst some of the other prominent people who performed the crowning.

Concert and sing-along at Dysart Cross, *c.*1946. These impromtu gatherings were a regular feature during the summer months and were very popular with the many Glaswegians who came here on holiday. On the accordion is Wullie Mathieson, and the fiddler is Wull Farquar.

Rosslyn Junior Football Club, 1929/30. From left to right, back row: J. Hardie, G. Barclay, J. Mill, G. Robertson, W. Mckay, R. Wilson. Middle row: W. Gillespie, D. Don, A. Mitchell, J. Pollock, D. Robertson, J. rae, P. Ronan, J. Lightfoot, D. Thomson (President). Front row: M. Grubb (Vice President), J. Philip (Match Secretary), D. Adams, F. Robertson, J. Penman, J. Sharp, J. Murphy, P. Hood, A. Low (Trainer). Formed in 1920, Rosslyn Juniors went on to become one of the most successful amateur teams in Scotland. In the 1928/29 season they lifted the League Cup, Fife Junior Cup and the Cowdenbeath Cup, becoming the first club to achieve this unique feat. Their pitch, Station Park, was in Windmill Road where Windmill Place is now. Several of the players went on to play professional football, among them, Jock Drysdale, who played for Manchester United, and Alan Bell, who played in goal for Scotland.

Right: John McDouall Stuart 1815–1866. John McDouall Stuart was born in Dysart on 7 September 1815. He trained as a civil engineer at the Scottish Naval and Military Academy in Edinburgh, and in 1838 sailed for Australia. Between 1858 and 1862 he led six expeditions into the centre of the continent, the last succeeding in crossing from south to north against the most arduous conditions imaginable. On his return to Adelaide, he and his team were hailed as heroes, but his health had been broken by his endeavours. He sailed for England in 1864 and died in London in 1866. He is buried at Kensal Green Cemetery.

Below: The birthplace of John McDouall Stuart, Rectory Lane, 1957. The house was restored and part of it was opened as a museum dedicated to Stuart, in 1977.

DYSART.

THE AULD SAUT BURGH BY THE SEA,
OF MEDIEVAL NAME,
DESERTA FROM THE HERMIT CELL,
SAINT SERF'S LONE SEA-CAVE HAME.

AS SUITOR LANG KIRKCALDY SOUGHT,
HER HAND FOR WEDDED JOY,
THE LASS HAS SILLER IN THE BANK,
AND THOUGH SHE'S OLD IS COY.

BY MAKIN' NAILS AND GUDE SEA SAUT,
SHE THROVE IN AULD LANGSYNE,
BENEATH THE TOWN AND FAR TO SEA,
SHE HAS HER GREAT COAL MINES.

THE HAVEN DOWN BELOW THE CLIFF,
THE SAILORS WALK, WE KEN;
THE TOWN HOUSE WI' ITS STANE ROOFED TOWER,
AND SERF'S KIRK BY THE GLEN.

"THE LORDLY LINE OF HIGH ST. CLAIR"
ARE STRANGERS TO THE LAND,
THOUGH DYSART HOUSE SO GREAT AND FAIR,
ALL STATELY YET DOTH STAND.

OLD RAVENSCRAIG IN RUINS NOW,
BRINGS BACK THE FEUDAL TIME,
OF ROSLIN'S EARLS AND ROSABELLE,
OF GOOD SIR WALTER'S RHYME.

THEN HEY! FOR DYSART'S CANTY CARLES,
AND LASSES A' SAE FINE,
THE STANE MAN CARVED OUT OF THE ROCK,
THE SAUT AND OCEAN MINE.

ANON. 1900.

Acknowledgements

The Society would like to thank the following people: John Irvine for his help with dates and details of people and places, Andrew Penman for his help with postcards and James Clunie (Peoples Institute).

Photograph of Adam Smith's painting on page 9 reproduced by kind permission of the Scottish National Portrait Galley—artist unknown.

Photograph of Robert Adam's painting on page 10 by courtesy of the National Portrait Gallery, London.

Photograph of Michael Beveridge's painting on page 11 by kind permission of Fife Council Museums, Kirkcaldy.

Photograph of Thomas Carlyle on page 12 reproduced by kind permission of Rare Books and Manuscripts, Columbia University.

Photograph of Anna Buchan on page 13 reproduced by kind permission of Hodder and Stoughton Limited.

Photograph of Pathhead Manse on page 13 reproduced by kind permission of the John Buchan Centre.

Thanks to all who made a contribution and to members of Kirkcaldy Civic Society for their enthusiastic work. Thanks also to Jim Swan from Dysart Trust for his hard work in the preparation of the last chapter of this book.